# The Family Parsha Book

MAGGID

RABBI SHALOM HAMMER

# THE FAMILY PARSHA BOOK

Maggid Books

*The Family Parsha Book*

First Maggid Edition, 2016

*Maggid Books*
*An imprint of Koren Publishers Jerusalem Ltd.*

POB 8531, New Milford, CT 06776-8531, USA
& POB 4044, Jerusalem 9104001, Israel
www.korenpub.com

The publication of this book was made possible
through the generous support of *Torah Education in Israel.*

ISBN 978-1-59264-428-5, *hardcover*
ISBN 978-1-59264-439-1, *paperback*

A CIP catalogue record for this title is
available from the British Library

Printed and bound in the United States

לכבוד חיילי צה״ל

Dedicated to

our son Yaakov who is serving in Nachal Brigade, Gedud 50,

and to all of the Soldiers of the IDF

whom I try to inspire every day and who inspire me incessantly.

״...לא בחיל ולא בכח כי אם ברוחי אמר ה׳ צבאות״ (זכריה פרק ד).

"…not through army and not through strength,
but through My spirit, said Hashem."

In honor of my dear father and teacher,

דוד יוסף בן יעקב יחיאל הלוי עמו״ש

Happy Birthday, Dad

ילכו מחיל לחיל יראה א-להים בציון

Thank You Hashem
for helping me find Gabi
and for granting us Bracha, Yakov Chaim, Adena,
Yakov (The Bear), Chamshush, Gili, and Sruli Boy

In honor of our Children and Grandchildren
**David and Maeve Samuels**

**Mr. Cecil Jowell**
thank you for your friendship and support

In honor of Jordy, Gabbi, and Lexie
**Dorothy and Leonard Sank**

In memory of Stanley and Audrey Bienenfeld's parents
**Julius Bienenfeld** יהודה אריה בן שלמה זאלי ז״ל
**Tessie Bienenfeld** טובה בת מתתיהו ז״ל

לזכר נשמות הורינו היקרים
אברהם משה בן הרב שלמה זאלי ז״ל וגוטקה טובה בת רב אברהם דוד ע״ה
למשפחת ביננפלד
יהודה לייב בן אהרון זאב ז״ל וחוה מינה בת יצחק אייזיק ע״ה
למשפחת יוסדן
מוקדש ע״י ר׳ מנחם שמואל והדסה ביננפלד

In loving memory of **Solly Tager** שאול בן אליהו זעליג הלוי ז״ל
a true physical and spiritual giant, whose love and kindness touched
the lives of many

In honor of our parents
**Rabbi David & Eileen Lesnick and Shaya & Rhona Bar Chama**
**Marc & Tamar Lesnick**

Sponsored by **Kim and Lance Katz**
in loving memory of their grandparents:
Samuel Velkes, Alf and Tilly Beerman, Yudel and Sylvia Katz, and
Saiah and Sarah Adelson

Dedicated to the memory
of my dear loving parents
**Dovid and Suri Schwartz A"H**
both of whom were survivors of the Holocaust
and both of whom never lost faith in Hashem.
Their mission instilled in their children, grandchildren,
great-grandchildren, and great-great-grandchildren,
Torah values, Chesed, and a love for Jews everywhere.
שלי שלכם!
Mendy and Lynn Schwartz New York

# Contents

11 | Preface
13 | Acknowledgments

15 | ספר בראשית
**Sefer Bereshit**

17 | בראשית Bereshit
21 | נח Noach
25 | לך לך Lech Lecha
29 | וירא Vayera
33 | חיי שרה Chayei Sara
37 | תולדות Toldot
41 | ויצא Vayetze
45 | וישלח Vayishlach
49 | וישב Vayeshev
53 | מקץ Miketz
57 | ויגש Vayigash
61 | ויחי Vayechi

65 | ספר שמות
**Sefer Shemot**

67 | שמות Shemot
71 | וארא Va'era
75 | בא Bo
79 | בשלח Beshalach
83 | יתרו Yitro
87 | משפטים Mishpatim
91 | תרומה Teruma
95 | תצוה Tetzave
99 | כי תישא Ki Tisa
103 | ויקהל Vayak'hel
107 | פקודי Pekudei

111 | ספר ויקרא
**Sefer Vayikra**

113 | ויקרא Vayikra
117 | צו Tzav

121 שמיני Shmini
125 תזריע מצורע Tazria Metzora
129 אחרי מות Acharei Mot
133 קדושים Kedoshim
137 אמור Emor
141 בהר Behar
145 בחוקותי Bechukotai

149 ספר במדבר
**Sefer Bamidbar**
151 במדבר Bamidbar
155 נשא Naso
159 בהעלותך Behaalotcha
163 שלח Shlach
167 קרח Korach
171 חוקת Chukat
175 בלק Balak
179 פנחס Pinchas
183 מטות Matot
187 מסעי Masei

191 ספר דברים
**Sefer Devarim**
193 דברים Devarim
197 ואתחנן Vaetchanan
201 עקב Ekev
205 ראה Re'eh
209 שופטים Shoftim
213 כי תצא Ki Tetze
217 כי תבוא Ki Tavo
221 נצבים Nitzavim
225 וילך Vayelech
229 האזינו Haazinu
233 וזאת הברכה Vezot HaBeracha

237 פתרונות Answer Key
285 מונחון Glossary

# Preface

**A**s a concerned educator and a father of six, I am always looking for ways to keep my children interested and involved at the Shabbat table. I want the Shabbat table to serve as the focal family meeting place and represent our commitment to Torah. A few years ago, I introduced my family to a Hebrew *sefer* which asked questions on the weekly parsha and whose answers followed an 'ב 'א sequence, whereby the first answer began with an 'א, the second answer with a 'ב, etc. I challenged my children to supply the answers while sitting around the Shabbat table and reviewing the parsha, using the *sefer* as the incentive. My children embraced the challenge and the questions became part of our Shabbat table ritual. Friends who joined us for the Shabbat meal were impressed by the learning exchange and interaction and they often commented on how nicely our children sat at the table. The 'ב 'א format encouraged my children because it provided helpful hints. Adults also found the *sefer* challenging and a useful way of reviewing the parsha. Through the encouragement of my wife, family, and friends, I decided that the format of such a positive learning tool should be available to facilitate all Jewish families and educators. I developed my own challenging questions and decided to make a more comprehensive *sefer*.

In addition to a review of *parshat hashavua, The Family Parsha Book* includes Haftorah Highlights, which explain the parsha's connection with the *haftorah,* as well as Parsha Puzzlers, which promote a thorough analysis of one of the main issues in each parsha. Some of the questions are demarcated with a star indicating that these questions are particularly challenging and following some of the questions are points of discussion on Jewish laws that relate to the answer. Reviewing these *halachot* helps demonstrate the connection between the Written and Oral Law.

When reviewing the questions, I highly recommend doing so with a *chumash* at hand. Many of the questions require reference to the *pasuk* and to Rashi's commentary. The cross-referencing helps improve reading skills and proficiency.

I pray that you will enjoy and benefit from this *sefer* as much as my family does, and *bezechut* the Torah advanced through it, may Hashem strengthen our commitment to Torah and our children's Jewish education.

# Acknowledgments

When I first contemplated working on this *sefer* it all seemed like a dream, and I most certainly never dreamed that I would be printing a third edition. There are many people I would like to thank without whose encouragement and help I would not have been able to write this *sefer*, let alone witness the printing of this third edition.

I want to thank Matthew Miller and Maggid Books for publishing this edition with such professionalism, and Daniel Rose and Tomi Mager for editing and overseeing the process through. It is always a pleasure to work with Maggid and I look forward to working on future projects together.

I would be remiss if I did not mention the people from whom it all began. To this day, I recall the Pesach Seder and visiting with my Bubie and Zadie. I can taste and smell the cooking, and the laughter I shared with them still resonates in my ears. Grandma demonstrated what it meant to work hard for *Kedushat Shabbat* and *Yom Tov*. Bubie, Zadie, and Grandma exemplified the importance of including one's children in what life has to offer. They nurtured the concept of Jewish family, which my parents clearly inherited.

My revered parents are exceptional examples who always emphasized the importance of family and spending time together in a religiously vigorous environment. They insisted that every Shabbat each one of their children share a *devar Torah* at the Shabbat table and lead the *zemirot Shabbat*. This is the essence of what this *sefer* encapsulates and what I hope it will encourage.

My beloved wife, Gabi, is my anchor. Patient, understanding, sensible, and practical, she is my best friend, teacher, and partner all at the same time.

Our dear children Bracha, Yakov Chaim, Adena, Yakov, The Chamshush, Gili, and Sruli Boy continue every day to remind me that, to quote someone I once knew, "When I look into their eyes I see eternity." I hope and pray that *bezchut* the learning promoted by this *sefer*, Hashem will watch over them and help strengthen their commitment to Torah and mitzvot.

Thank you Tobin and Waxman families for consistently sampling my questions on Shabbat and offering insights and feedback; you are both tremendous sources of support.

There are a number of friends and relatives who have consistently been supportive of my projects and graciously contributed towards the printing of this third edition. Those are my dear friends from Cape Town, David and Maeve Samuels (David…I spelled it right!), Leonard and Dorothy Sank, Lance and Kim Katz, Cecil Jowell, and Jonny Tager and the Tager family. I wish to thank my cousins Marvin and Dasi Bienenfeld and Stanley and Audrey Bienenfeld, my friends Marc and Tamar Lesnick, and Mendy and Lynn Schwartz.

May Hashem grant all of you and your families much *nachas bezchut* the support you all demonstrate on behalf of the Jewish community and Eretz Yisrael.

וראה בנים לבניך שלום על ישראל

Shalom Hammer

# ספר בראשית

# SEFER BERESHIT

# בראשית
# BERESHIT

**Parsha Points:**

▶ During the Six Days of Creation Hashem created the world. He separated between light and darkness. He created the שמים and the ארץ; the oceans, sun, moon, and all of the stars; the animals and fish; and finally, man and woman.

▶ On the seventh day Hashem stopped creating and rested. This day of rest is called Shabbat. On Shabbat, Jews rest and reflect on their relationship with Hashem.

▶ Adam and Chava sinned and were banished from Gan Eden.

▶ Two of the sons of Adam and Chava were Kayin and Hevel. They offered sacrifices to Hashem. Hashem accepted Hevel's sacrifice and rejected Kayin's. Out of jealousy, Kayin killed his brother Hevel and was punished.

▶ The parsha records the lineage and families of the children of Adam and Chava and their descendants.

Questions

א  We know that Hashem was by Himself on the first day of Creation because it says: ██████ ויהי ערב ויהי בקר יום. (Rashi, 1:5)

ב  Hashem did not allow the first few generations to eat ██████.

ג  The Midrash says that כי טוב is not written on the second day of Creation because on that day ██████ was created.

ד  The two abilities that man has and animals lack are ██████ and ██████.

> Discuss which ברכות in תפילה thank Hashem for דעת and דיבור. Give examples of times when we use our mouths unproductively. How can we use our power of speech more constructively?

ה  ██████ was killed by his brother.

ו  What does it say in the Torah at the end of each day of Creation?

ז  Hashem told Adam that he can eat from all עשב that is ██████.

ח  Which of Kayin's sons died young?

ט *  How does the פסוק say that the עשב of the field, "did not yet bear fruit?" (2:5)

י  Hashem said ██████, and then there was light.

ב On the third day of Creation it says ▨▨▨ ▨▨▨ twice.

ל* Who killed his own grandfather and son by mistake?

מ* The two creations that were upset because they were far away from Hashem were the ▨▨▨ and the ▨▨▨. Hashem added them into the ingredients of the ▨▨▨.

Discuss what a קרבן מנחה is and when it is offered.

נ What was Kayin's punishment?

ס* The Torah says יום הששי because the whole world was created in order to give the Torah on the sixth day of which month? (Rashi, 1:31)

ע* Hashem created a wife for Adam so she could be an ▨▨▨ ▨▨▨.

פ Kayin brought זרע ▨▨▨ as a קרבן to Hashem. (4:3)

צ Hashem created Chava out of Adam's ▨▨▨.

ק* Where did Adam go to after he was thrown out of Gan Eden? (Rashi, 4:16)

ר What was Hevel's job?

ש Which of Adam's sons populated the world?

ת What kind of tree was the עץ הדעת?

**Parsha Puzzler**

Why does the Torah start with the creation of the world? Why not begin the Torah with קידוש החודש, the first mitzva the Jewish people were commanded as a nation?

**Haftorah Highlights**

The Torah begins by telling us that Hashem created the שמים and the ארץ. This teaches us that every Jew's commitment to the Torah begins with אמונה בה׳. In the *haftorah*, the *navi* Yeshayahu reminds Benei Yisrael of this same thing. Yeshayahu encourages Benei Yisrael to live their lives with אמונה בה׳ by doing the mitzvot of the Torah. (*Yeshayahu* 42:5–43:10)

**Learning Lesson**

Hashem saw that Adam was lonely so He created Chava to be his wife. After Adam ate from the עץ הדעת he complained to Hashem about Chava and blamed her for his own sin. The Gemara says that Adam did not appreciate what was given to him. It is important to recognize what Hashem gives us and to be grateful for the people closest to us.

**Parsha Points:**

▶ There were many bad people living in the generations after Adam and Chava.

▶ Hashem decides to bring a מבול that would destroy the world, but He decides to save the lives of Noach, who was a צדיק, his family, and the animals.

▶ Noach builds a תיבה to save his family and the animals. When the מבול begins, they go in the תיבה and are saved. The rest of the world is destroyed.

▶ After the מבול stops, Noach and everything in the תיבה exit.

▶ Noach offers קורבנות to Hashem, and Hashem promises Noach that He will never bring another מבול upon the world again.

## Questions

א\*   Who bit Noach because he did not get his food on time?

ב   If the people did תשובה, then the rain would become גשמי ▒▒▒▒. (Rashi, 7:12)

> Discuss what תשובה is, how it is done, and why it is effective.

ג   What was the תיבה made out of, and why? (Rashi, 6:14)

ד   Which life forms were not punished in the מבול?

ה   Which word in the parsha is written one way but read a different way, and why? (Rashi, 8:17)

ו\*   From which phrase in the parsha does Hashem demonstrate to judges that they should not pass judgment until they have complete understanding? (11:5)

ז   What covered Moshe's תיבה, and why? (Rashi, 6:14)

ח   The דור המבול was punished because they filled the world with ▒▒▒▒.

ט   Seven of this type of animal were put onto the תיבה.

י\*   What is another word in the parsha for "all of existence"?

כ   What did Noach plant when he came out of the תיבה?

> With which mitzvot do we use wine, and why?

ל\*   What did Hashem promise the people of the world after the מבול?

מ   The Hebrew word for an animal species is ▆▆▆▆.

נ   Who was Cham's grandson, and what did he do? (Rashi, 10:8)

ס   Why was  Sara called יסכה? (Rashi, 11:29)

ע   This bird never did what he was sent to do.

פ   The mitzva to have children is called ▆▆▆▆.

צ *  What was the window in the תיבה called, and why?

ק   This was a sign used to show that Hashem made a ברית not to destroy the world again.

What ברכה do we make when we see the קשת?

ר   Which animal was too big to fit into the תיבה?

ש   Who was Noach's son?

ת   Nine generations after Noach, ▆▆▆▆ was born, and he was ▆▆▆▆'s father.

Why did Hashem destroy the world if the Torah wasn't given yet and people did not know how to behave properly?

The מבול destroyed the world, but it was also an opportunity to rebuild a better world. The *navi* Yeshayahu told Benei Yisrael that tragedies such as the מבול, the חורבן הבית, and the גלות have a purpose. Their purpose is to encourage תשובה and strengthen Benei Yisrael's commitment to Hashem. (*Yeshayahu* 54:1–55:5)

The Midrash says that Noach and his sons did not sleep for an entire year because they had to take care of the animals in the תיבה. This sensitivity and care that Noach and his sons demonstrated were very important qualities for the world to learn. If Noach and his sons treated the animals so carefully, certainly we should be thoughtful and considerate of the people around us.

# לך לך
# LECH LECHA

▶ Avram believes in Hashem.

▶ Hashem tells Avram and his wife, Sarai, to leave their home and go to Eretz Canaan.

▶ There is a famine in Canaan and Avram, Sarai, and Avram's nephew Lot go to Mitzrayim, where they find food and fortune.

▶ Avram leaves Mitzrayim and goes to Canaan. Lot leaves Avram and goes to Sedom.

▶ In the ברית בין הבתרים, Hashem makes a ברית with Avram and changes Avram's name to Avraham. He also promises Avraham that he will have many descendants, and that he and his descendants will inherit Eretz Yisrael.

Questions

א    Avram's name was changed to ▨▨▨▨. (17:5)

ב    What was the name of the ברית that Hashem made with Avraham in the parsha?

ג    Hashem told Avraham that his children would be ▨▨▨▨ when they go down to Mitzrayim.

ד*    Avram's servant Eliezer was from ▨▨▨▨. (Rashi, 15:2)

ה    Who felt that it is better to be a slave in the house of Avraham than a princess in a palace?

ו    Which word means that Hashem punished Pharaoh? (12:17)

ז    Hashem promised Avraham that ▨▨▨▨ would multiply like the dust on the earth.

> Explain the true meaning of this ברכה. Discuss times throughout Jewish history when the גוים persecuted us but we managed to survive.

ח*    Avraham refused to take even a ▨▨▨▨ from the king of Sedom.

ט*    How many animals did Avraham use for the ברית בין הבתרים, and which animals were they?

י    Who received a ברית מילה when he was thirteen years old?

> On which day is a ברית מילה performed? Can it be performed on Shabbat? What ברכה is made on a ברית מילה?

כ   Who was the strongest king from the four nations that Avraham fought?

ל   Avraham's nephew was ▨▨▨▨.

מ   What was the name of the king of Shalem who greeted Avraham with bread and wine?

נ *   Hashem promised Avraham that the land from ▨▨▨▨ until ▨▨▨▨ would belong to the Jewish people.

ס   Lot left Avraham and went to live in ▨▨▨▨.

ע *   At what time of day did Avraham give himself and all the men and boys living in his house a ברית מילה?

פ   Avraham told Sara to pretend that she was his sister to protect her from ▨▨▨▨.

צ   The first direction that Hashem told Avraham to see Eretz Yisrael from was ▨▨▨▨. (13:17)

ק *   Avraham would be ▨▨▨▨ years old when Sara gave birth to a son.

ר   The ▨▨▨▨ of Avraham fought with the ▨▨▨▨ of Lot.

ש   Hashem changed ▨▨▨▨'s name to ▨▨▨▨.

ת   What were the two birds that Avraham took for the ברית בין הבתרים?

**Parsha Puzzler**

How did Avraham become the first person to believe in Hashem?

**Haftorah Highlights**

Avraham's חסד is shown to us all throughout the parsha. In the *haftorah*, the *navi* Yeshayahu encourages Benei Yisrael to return to Hashem by performing חסד and following the example of Avraham Avinu. As a result of Avraham's character, Hashem promises him that he will become a great nation. Yeshayahu calls Benei Yisrael the descendants of Avraham, and tells them that if they believe in Hashem and are kind to one another, they too will become a great nation. (*Yeshayahu* 40:27–41:16)

**Learning Lesson**

The Midrash says that Avraham looked at a city and asked, "Is it possible for a city to have lights without someone lighting up the city?" It was then that Hashem appeared to Avraham. This teaches us that Avraham found Hashem because he was searching for Him. Sometimes we may feel that Hashem is not with us. If we continue to ask questions and look for Hashem, we will notice that He really is near after all.

# VAYERA

Parsha Points:

- Avraham gives himself and every man and boy living in his house a ברית מילה.

- Three מלאכים come to visit Avraham as he recovers from his ברית מילה. One of the מלאכים informs Avraham and Sara that they will have a son.

- One of the מלאכים is sent to destroy Sedom for its wickedness, and the other one is sent to save Lot and his family and rescue them from Sedom.

- Sara gives birth to Yitzchak. She sends Hagar and Yishmael out of her house because she fears the bad influence Yishmael has on Yitzchak.

- Hashem tests Avraham by instructing him to sacrifice his son Yitzchak to Him. Avraham listens to Hashem and is ready to fulfill the request. A מלאך stops Avraham from doing so. This demonstration of Avraham's servitude to Hashem is called עקידת יצחק.

Questions

א    Where did Hashem appear to Avraham? (Rashi, 18:1)

ב    Which mitzva do we learn from Hashem in the parsha?

ג    Hashem promised Avraham that he would become a ▭▭▭ ▭▭▭ .

ד    The people of Sedom came to Lot's house and wanted to break down his ▭▭▭ . (19:9)

ה    Who was afraid that her son would die in the desert?

ו    Which words teach us that Avraham was anxious to perform the mitzvot of Hashem by himself and not through a messenger? (Rashi, 22:3)

> Discuss which mitzvot can be done through a messenger and which cannot.

ז    Which important idea do we learn from the way Avraham ran to do mitzvot?

> Demonstrate how our days are filled with opportunities to do mitzvot.

ח    One of the foods that Avraham offered the מלאכים was ▭▭▭ .

ט    Sedom was destroyed because the people there did not have ▭▭▭ מדות.

> Discuss what it means to have מדות טובות. Give examples, and explain their importance.

י    Avraham sacrificed an איל in place of ▭▭▭ .

כ    Hashem promised Avraham that Benei Yisrael would be like the ▓▓▓▓▓ ▓▓▓▓▓.

ל    Which part of the animal did Avraham offer to each one of the מלאכים (his guests)? (Rashi, 18:7)

מ *    What was the knife that Avraham used for עקידת יצחק called?

נ *    Yishmael is also referred to in the parsha as the ▓▓▓▓▓. (Rashi, 18:7)

ס    In this week's parsha, we learn that you have to eat bread in order to make a ▓▓▓▓▓.

> Discuss the *halachot* of המוציא, נטילת ידים, and ברכת המזון. When do you have to wash your hands? Which ברכה do you make? How much bread do you have to eat in order to say ברכת המזון? What is לחם משנה? How do we know that ברכת המזון is from the Torah?

ע    What are the two nations that come from Lot?

פ    On which festival did the מלאכים come to visit Avraham?

צ    From Sara we learn how important it is to be ▓▓▓▓▓.

ק    How did Hashem command Avraham to sacrifice Yitzchak? (22:2)

> Discuss what צניעות is and why it is so important. Demonstrate how we preserve צניעות in and out of our homes, through both the way we dress and the way we behave.

ר    Betuel had a daughter whose name was ▓▓▓▓▓.

ש    Avraham ran out to greet ▓▓▓▓▓.

ת    Where did Avraham tell the מלאכים to sit?

## Parsha Puzzler

Why did Sara laugh when the מלאך told Avraham that she would have a son? Did Sara doubt what Hashem promised?

## Haftorah Highlights

At the beginning of the parsha, Avraham waits patiently in the heat of the day to invite people into his home. Hashem sends Avraham guests who serve as His messengers. The *haftorah* begins by introducing a woman who desperately needs help. Hashem sends the *navi* Elisha as His messenger in order to help the woman. The parsha and the *haftorah* display the חסד of both Avraham and Elisha, who want to do Hashem's mitzvot. (*II Melachim* 4:1–37)

## Learning Lesson

Avraham Avinu sat outside his tent looking for guests, he prayed to Hashem to save the people of Sedom, he gave a ברית מילה to himself and to every man and boy in his entire household, and he took his son Yitzchak to Har Ha-Moriya and was prepared to sacrifice him to Hashem. The Gemara says that Avraham did more than what he said he would do, because he was always involved in performing mitzvot. Let's follow Avraham's example and look for opportunities to do mitzvot, such as helping our parents, giving צדקה, or visiting the sick. There are mitzvot around us constantly, waiting to be fulfilled.

# CHAYEI SARA

**Parsha Points:**

▶ Sara Imenu dies and Avraham buries her in Maarat Ha-Machpela.

▶ Avraham sends his servant Eliezer to find a wife for Yitzchak.

▶ Eliezer is impressed with Rivka. Rivka demonstrates sensitivity and kindness as she feeds both Eliezer and his camels.

▶ Eliezer convinces Betuel, Rivka's father, and Lavan, Rivka's brother, to allow her to marry Yitzchak. Yitzchak marries Rivka.

▶ At the end of the parsha, Avraham Avinu dies.

Questions

א * Who were the first people to be buried in Maarat HaMachpela? (Rashi, 23:2)

ב The Torah says that Hashem blessed Avraham _____. This means that Avraham had a _____ (Rashi, 24:1)

ג When Rivka saw Yitzchak for the first time, she made herself fall off of the _____.

ד * Eliezer prayed that _____ ה׳ מצליח.

ה Both Lavan and Betuel said that the marriage of Rivka to Yitzchak was from _____. (24:50)

ו Which פסוק teaches us that Yitzchak prayed תפילת מנחה?

What are the *halachot* of מנחה? During which time of day can one pray מנחה? Can one eat before מנחה?

ז Eliezer is also referred to as the _____ of Avraham.

ח What is the name of the city where Sara died?

ט * When Eliezer heard that Rivka would marry Yitzchak he bowed down. We learn from this that you have to thank Hashem for _____ בשורות. (Rashi, 24:52)

י Yitzchak and _____ buried Avraham together.

כ Avraham made Eliezer promise that he would not find a wife for Yitzchak from the nation of _____.

ל Who was Rivka's brother?

מ  Avraham bought ▨▨▨▨▨ ▨▨▨▨▨ from עפרון.

נ  The Torah calls Rivka a ▨▨▨▨▨. (24:16)

ס  At the end of the parsha, the Torah tells us the ▨▨▨▨▨ of Yishmael's lineage. (Rashi, 25:13)

ע  Eliezer was Avraham's ▨▨▨▨▨.

פ *  Avraham gave gifts to the sons of the ▨▨▨▨▨.

צ  What jewelry was given to Rivka as a gift?

ק  What is another name for הגר, and why? (Rashi, 25:1)

ר *  The ברכה that Lavan gave to Rivka when she left her father's house was ▨▨▨▨▨ אחותנו את היי לאלפי.

ש *  What did Avraham use to buy Maarat HaMachpela?

ת *  Avraham called himself a גר and a ▨▨▨▨▨.

**Parsha Puzzler**

Why was it so important for Avraham to buy Maarat HaMachpela and bury Sara there?

**Haftorah Highlights**

In this parsha, Avraham Avinu makes preparations as he nears the end of his life. Avraham wants to find the right wife for his son Yitzchak in order to ensure the future of Am Yisrael. In the *haftorah*, David Ha-Melech is also near the end of his life. He prepares his son Shlomo to take over the kingdom for the sake of his family and the Jewish people. (*I Melachim* 1:1–31)

**Learning Lesson**

Avraham calls himself a גר and a תושב (23:4). A גר is a stranger and a תושב is a permanent resident. How can Avraham be both of these at once? Rav Shlomo Aviner suggests that Avraham is describing the philosophy of the Jewish people. While we live in the physical world we are גרים because everything material is temporary. The spiritual world is permanent because it is the world of truth. We should strengthen our connection to it and become "permanent residents" of רוחניות by performing mitzvot.

# תּוֹלְדוֹת
# TOLDOT

▷ Yitzchak and Rivka have twin sons named Yaakov and Esav.

▷ When the twins are older, Esav sells his birthright to Yaakov.

▷ Yaakov receives the birthright ברכה from Yitzchak and, as instructed by Rivka, he then flees to the home of Lavan.

▷ When Esav finds out that Yaakov received the ברכה, he threatens to find Yaakov and kill him.

Questions

א   What color was Esav when he was born?

ב   Esav sold the ▒▒▒▒▒ to Yaakov.

ג   Hashem told Rivka that there are two ▒▒▒▒▒ in her womb.

ד   Part of the ברכה that Yitzchak gave to Yaakov is that he would have a lot of ▒▒▒▒▒. (27:28)

ה*   How did Esav tell Yaakov to feed him? (25:30)

ו   What is another word used in the parsha for תפילה?

ז*   When Yitzchak was ▒▒▒▒▒, he could not see that well.

ח*   After Yaakov received the ברכה from Yitzchak, where did Rivka tell Yaakov to run to?

ט*   Yitzchak's first ברכה was that Hashem should provide Yaakov with ▒▒▒▒▒ from the שמים.

> Discuss תפילת טל: When it is recited, and why at that particular time of year? What are the different מנהגים with regard to reciting מוריד הטל in the שמונה עשרה? What is the *halacha* if someone forgets to say מוריד הטל in the שמונה עשרה?

י   Which words in the פסוק show that Yaakov studied Torah? (25:27)

> Discuss the mitzva of תלמוד תורה. How do we know that one is obligated to study Torah?

כ After Yaakov left Yitzchak's house, he did not return home for ⬛⬛⬛⬛ years. (Rashi, 28:9)

ל What was one of the things that Yaakov offered Esav to eat?

מ How did Yaakov ask Esav for the בכורה?

נ* Whose sister did Esav marry?

ס What did the Pelishtim do to the wells that Yitzchak dug?

ע* Yitzchak said he could not leave Eretz Yisrael because he was an ⬛⬛⬛⬛ ⬛⬛⬛⬛.

פ* Which city did Yitzchak send Yaakov to?

צ* Esav was a good ⬛⬛⬛⬛.

ק Yitzchak recognized Yaakov's ⬛⬛⬛⬛ when he came to get the ברכה.

ר What is one of the names of the wells that Yitzchak dug that is still a city in Eretz Yisrael today?

List cities mentioned in the Torah that are currently part of Eretz Yisrael.

ש Esav came from the ⬛⬛⬛⬛, and he was tired and hungry.

ת Yaakov is described as an ⬛⬛⬛⬛ איש.

**Parsha Puzzler**

Did Yitzchak prefer to give the ברכות to Esav rather than Yaakov, and if so, why?

**Haftorah Highlights**

The parsha describes Esav as a רשע who worshiped עבודה זרה and, in contrast, his brother, Yaakov, who was a צדיק and an עבד ה'. Yaakov and Esav are two nations who are totally opposite from one another. The beginning of the *haftorah* mentions Yaakov and Esav and the differences between the nations of Yisrael and Edom. Benei Yisrael must follow Yaakov's example of רוחניות, similar to the one described for the Kohanim in the *haftorah*. (*Malachi* 1:1–2:7)

**Learning Lesson**

The בכורה gave Yaakov the right to inherit Avraham and Yitzchak's ברכות for all future generations. Esav gave his birthright to Yaakov in exchange for something to eat. Esav sacrificed his future for the sake of his immediate needs. Even if we feel that we need something right away, if we control ourselves, we will recognize the benefit of being patient.

# VAYETZE

**Parsha Points:**

▶ On his way to the house of Lavan, Yaakov stops to sleep and has a dream. Yaakov dreams of a ladder that goes from the ארץ to the שמים above, with מלאכים ascending and descending. When Yaakov awakens, he offers קרבנות to Hashem. Hashem promises Eretz Yisrael to Yaakov and his children.

▶ Yaakov goes to Charan and works for Lavan. Lavan has two daughters, Leah and Rachel. Yaakov works seven years for each daughter and marries them both.

▶ Leah gives birth to four sons. Bilha and Zilpa give birth to two sons each. Although at first Rachel cannot bear a child, Hashem answers her prayers and she gives birth to Yosef.

▶ Yaakov and his entire family leave Lavan's house to return to Eretz Canaan.

# Questions

א* How many of the שבטים are born in the parsha?

ב Yaakov met Rachel at the ________.

ג Yaakov called the memorial to his covenant with Lavan ________. (31:47)

ד* What did Reuven give to his mother Leah?

ה Why did Leah call her son Yehuda?

ו How do we know that Yaakov prayed תפילת ערבית? (Rashi, 28:11)

> Discuss the *halachot* of מעריב. During which time frame can one pray מעריב?

ז Leah's sixth son was named ________.

ח At the beginning of the parsha, Yaakov lies down and has a ________.

ט An animal that is killed by another animal is called a ________. (31:39)

י How does the Torah describe Rachel? (29:17)

כ* Levi was given the ________ presents of the ________. (Rashi, 29:34)

ל Whose eyes are described in the parsha?

מ What did Lavan place as a boundary between him and Yaakov?

נ    Lavan gave Yaakov a _____ to see if he had diamonds in his mouth. (Rashi, 29:13)

ס    Before Yaakov went to sleep, he took the stones and placed them _____. (Rashi, 28:11)

ע    Yaakov did seven extra years of _____ for Lavan in order to marry Rachel.

פ    From where did Yaakov lift a large stone?

צ    For twenty years, Yaakov looked after the _____ of Lavan.

ק    Lavan's older daughter was Leah, and Rachel was the _____.

ר *    What was the name of Leah's oldest son, and why?

ש    Bilha and Zilpa were _____.

ת *    What is another word for idols that is found in this week's parsha?

## Parsha Puzzler

Why did Yaakov kiss Rachel and then cry when he first saw her?

## Haftorah Highlights

Yaakov Avinu faced many difficulties in his life, but he always recognized Hashem above. In the *haftorah*, the *navi* Hoshea refers to some of the events that happened to Yaakov in the parsha. Hoshea reprimanded Benei Yisrael for worshiping עבודה זרה, and he told them that even when they face difficulties, they should follow Yaakov's example and continue to believe in Hashem. (*Hoshea* 12:13–14:10 [*Yoel* 2:26–27; *Hoshea* 11:7–12:12])

## Learning Lesson

The Torah says that when Rachel saw that Leah had children she was jealous of her. The Midrash explains that Rachel was not jealous of Leah herself, but of her מדות. Rachel thought that if Leah could have children, then she must be a צדקת and worth learning from. Jealousy is a negative מידה. When we see people who have more than us, let's avoid jealous feelings by concentrating on their מדות טובות.

# וישלח
# VAYISHLACH

**Parsha Points:**

▷ On his way to Eretz Canaan, Yaakov prepares his family for a confrontation with Esav.

▷ Before Yaakov confronts Esav, he struggles with a מלאך ה׳, and his name is changed to Yisrael.

▷ Yaakov confronts Esav, and Esav's anger is appeased. Following the meeting, Rachel dies.

▷ Yaakov settles in Eretz Canaan.

Questions

א   In which direction did Yaakov send מלאכים?

ב   Which of Yaakov's sons was born in this week's parsha?

ג   What part of the animal is prohibited to eat?

ד   Who was taken captive by Shechem?

ה   What did R. Shimon bar Yochai say about the meeting between Yaakov and Esav? (Rashi, 33:4)

ו   Which word is used to show that the person who died was a צדיק? (35:29)

ז   Yaakov's sons told Shechem that they should circumcise all of the ▓▓▓▓.

ח *   What did Yaakov do to his family before they met Esav?

ט   Yaakov ▓▓▓▓ all of the idols that were taken from Shechem. (35:4)

י   What is the other name that is given to Yaakov in the parsha?

כ   The מלאך touched Yaakov on ▓▓▓▓.

ל   Who was the mother of Reuven, Shimon, Levi, Yehuda, Yissachar, and Zevulun?

מ   How old was Yitzchak when he died?

נ *   What is on top of the word וישקהו, and why? (Rashi, 33:4)

ס    Which place that Yaakov traveled to has the same name as a Jewish festival?

ע    Yaakov refers to himself as Esav's ▬▬▬▬ to make Esav feel good. (32:5)

פ *    Where did Yaakov struggle with a מלאך?

צ    After Yaakov fought with the מלאך, he was ▬▬▬▬. (32:32)

ק *    How does Yaakov say that his זכויות with Hashem are few?

ר    Who was the last person to introduce themselves to Esav?

ש *    In what state did Yaakov arrive in Shechem? (Rashi, 33:18)

ת    Yaakov lived with Lavan and still kept all of the מצות ▬▬▬▬. (Rashi, 32:5)

**Parsha Puzzler**

How did Yaakov arrange his family in preparation for the meeting with Esav, and why? What did Yosef do, and why? Why didn't Yaakov do this as well?

**Haftorah Highlights**

פרשת
וישלח
describes Yaakov's fear of meeting Esav after many years of separation. The *haftorah* says that Esav's nation, Edom, will always be a threat to Benei Yisrael's existence. Benei Yisrael will be saved from Edom, who will recognize the mistakes of Esav and the greatness of Yaakov. This will mark the beginning of our גאולה, as the *haftorah* ends with the פסוק that we say in our תפילה: ועלו מושיעים בהר ציון לשפוט את הר עשיו והיתה לה' המלוכה. (*Ovadyah* 1:1–21)

**Learning Lesson**

When Esav meets Yaakov, he says יש לי רב – I have a lot. Yaakov, on the other hand, says יש לי כל – I have everything. Esav may have been wealthier than Yaakov, but Yaakov felt that he had everything. We should follow Yaakov's example and be שמח בחלקו – happy with what we have.

# VAYESHEV

## Parsha Points:

▶ Yaakov shows favor to Yosef by making him the כתנת פסים.

▶ Yosef tells his father and his brothers of the dreams he had which show that they will all bow down to him.

▶ Yosef's brothers are jealous of him, and they throw him into a pit. Afterward, the brothers sell Yosef into slavery, and he is brought to Mitzrayim. The brothers inform Yaakov that Yosef was killed.

▶ Yosef works in Mitzrayim for Potiphar. Potiphar's wife complains about Yosef, and he is thrown in jail.

▶ In jail, Yosef meets Pharaoh's butler and baker and interprets dreams that they had.

Questions

א  In his first dream, Yosef dreamt about ▒▒▒▒▒ in the field.

ב  Yosef's brothers threw him into a ▒▒▒▒▒.

ג  What did the שר המשקים, the butler, dream about?

ד  What did Yosef bring in front of his father? (37:2)

ה  Which word in the parsha shows that Tamar was pregnant? (Rashi, 38:24)

ו  Which word in the parsha teaches us that Yosef placed בטחון in a man instead of having more בטחון in Hashem? (Rashi, 40:23)

List examples of events and people in our surroundings that help strengthen our בטחון in Hashem.

ז *  Yosef was born when Yaakov was old, and so he was called a ▒▒▒▒▒ בן. (Rashi, 37:3)

ח *  When Yosef was in jail, Hashem blessed him with ▒▒▒▒▒.

ט  How did Yaakov say that Yosef had been killed after the brothers showed him Yosef's coat? (37:33)

י  Who suggested selling Yosef to the Yishma'elim?

כ  What did Yaakov give only to Yosef?

ל *  Yosef spoke ▒▒▒▒▒ about his brothers.

Discuss the *halachot* of לשון הרע. What is the difference between לשון הרע and רכילות? What are different excuses that we use in order to talk לשון הרע? How can we better avoid לשון הרע?

מ   Whom was Yosef sold to before he was sold to the Yishma'elim?

נ*  At the beginning of the parsha, Yosef is described as a ▓▓▓▓▓.

ס   What did the שר האופים, the baker, carry on his head in his dream?

ע   What did Potiphar's wife place on Yosef? (39:7)

פ   Yosef worked in Mitzrayim for ▓▓▓▓▓.

צ*  Yehuda admitted that Tamar was ▓▓▓▓▓ ▓▓▓▓▓.

ק   All of the brothers had ▓▓▓▓▓ toward Yosef.

ר   Whose idea was it to throw Yosef into the בור, and not to kill him?

ש   Where did Yosef go to meet his brothers?

ת   She was prepared to be killed in order not to embarrass Yehuda. (Rashi, 38:25)

**Parsha Puzzler**

Was Yaakov wrong for favoring Yosef over his other sons? Why did the brothers want to kill Yosef, and how could they do this to their brother?

**Haftorah Highlights**

Amos reprimanded Benei Yisrael for showing hatred toward one another. Benei Yisrael were warned not to mistreat each other the way Benei Yaakov mistreated Yosef by selling him into slavery. (*Amos* 2:6–3:8)

**Learning Lesson**

Yehuda, who was a great תלמיד חכם, misjudged Tamar. When he realized that he was mistaken, he proclaimed "צדקה ממני," acknowledging his error. צדיקים make mistakes, and their greatness is that they admit when they are wrong and learn from their experiences. Don't be afraid of making mistakes; try to improve yourself by learning from them.

# מקץ
# MIKETZ

**Parsha Points:**

▶ Pharaoh has two disturbing dreams, and he calls upon Yosef to interpret them. After Yosef successfully does so, he becomes the second in command of Mitzrayim.

▶ There is a famine in Eretz Canaan, and Yaakov sends his sons to Mitzrayim for food. When Yosef's brothers arrive, he recognizes them, but they do not recognize him. Yosef demands that the brothers bring Binyamin, the youngest brother, to Mitzrayim as well. The brothers return to Canaan and Yehuda promises Yaakov that he will care for Binyamin in Mitzrayim. Yaakov agrees to Yehuda's suggestion, and Yehuda brings Binyamin to Mitzrayim.

▶ Yosef plants a silver cup in Binyamin's sack and accuses him of stealing it. Yosef tells the brothers that Binyamin will be placed in jail and that they should return to Yaakov.

Questions

א   Who was Yosef's wife?

ב   How does the Torah describe the seven fat cows in Pharaoh's dream?

ג   What did Yosef put in Binyamin's bag?

ד   How does the Torah describe the seven skinny cows?

ה   The brothers did not know who Yosef was and they called him ▬▬▬▬ whenever they spoke about him. (42:30)

ו*  Which word shows that Yosef pretended that he did not know who his brothers were, in order to teach them a lesson? (Rashi, 42:7)

ז   Pharaoh gave Yosef a chain made out of ▬▬▬▬.

ח   When Yosef recognized his brothers he knew that his ▬▬▬▬ would come true. (Rashi, 42:9)

ט   Pharaoh dreamt about ▬▬▬▬ שבע פרות that would represent שבע שנים ▬▬▬▬.

י   Who promised Yaakov that he would take care of Binyamin when they go down to Mitzrayim?

כ   What did each one of the brothers find in his bags?

ל   What did Pharaoh tell all of Mitzrayim after Yosef interpreted his dreams? (41:55)

מ   Who was Yosef's eldest son?

נ   How does the Torah say that Yosef felt bad for his brothers?

ס   The seven healthy cows that Pharaoh saw in his dream were a ▒▒▒▒ that there would be plenty of food in Mitzrayim during those seven years. (Rashi, 41:2)

ע   When Yosef found the goblet in Binyamin's bag, he said that Binyamin would have to become his ▒▒▒▒.

פ   Yosef was able to ▒▒▒▒ Pharaoh's dreams.

צ   What did Pharaoh call Yosef?

ק*  Yosef pretended that he did not know his brothers and spoke to them ▒▒▒▒.

ר   Yaakov sent his sons to Mitzrayim because there was a ▒▒▒▒ in Canaan.

ש   Which brother did Yosef place in prison?

ת*  Which word in the parsha means to understand and interpret dreams? (Rashi, 41:15)

## Parsha Puzzler

Why didn't Yosef reveal himself to his brothers, and why did he set them up to look like thieves?

## Haftorah Highlights

The parsha and the *haftorah* describe the dreams of two kings from two different nations. Pharaoh's dream shows that he was worried about the famine and his kingdom's survival; both of these concerns have to do with גשמיות – materialism. Shlomo's dream had to do with רוחניות – spirituality and his desire to serve Benei Yisrael with justice and righteousness. (*I Melachim* 3:15–4:1)

## Learning Lesson

Yosef was placed in prison for reasons that were unclear to him. While Yosef sat in jail, Pharaoh had disturbing dreams so that the שר המשקים would remember Yosef, the dream interpreter. The purpose of these events was to make Yosef a powerful ruler in Mitzrayim. We cannot always understand why things happen to us, but sometimes in the long run we may realize Hashem's plan.

# ויגש

# VAYIGASH

**Parsha Points:**

▷ Yehuda challenges Yosef and tells him that he will not leave Binyamin in Mitzrayim.

▷ Yosef reveals who he is. The brothers are embarrassed and ask for forgiveness. Yosef and his brothers are reunited.

▷ Yosef sends for his father to join them in Mitzrayim.

Questions

א    Yaakov did not want Binyamin to go down to Mitzrayim because maybe an ▨▨▨▨ would happen to him.

ב *    After Yosef told his brothers who he was, they could not answer him because they felt ▨▨▨▨. (Rashi, 46:3)

> Discuss the consequences of embarrassing someone in public. Why is it considered like killing someone?

ג    In which land did Yaakov and his sons settle in Mitzrayim?

ד *    First Yosef spoke to the brothers, then ▨▨▨▨ ▨▨▨▨ ▨▨▨▨ because they were embarrassed to speak to him first.

ה    What was the first question Yosef asked his brothers after he revealed himself?

ו    What did Yosef do to each one of his brothers?

ז    On the way down to Mitzrayim, Yaakov stopped in Be'er Sheva to offer ▨▨▨▨. (46:1)

ח    Yosef gave ▨▨▨▨ to each of his brothers.

ט    What is another word for children in the parsha? (45:19)

י    Which brother was sent to Goshen first?

כ    Yosef gave Binyamin three hundred pieces of ▨▨▨▨.

ל    Gershon, Kehat, and Merari were the sons of ▨▨▨▨.

מ *    Yosef saw that the ▨▨▨▨ was in Binyamin's portion of Eretz Yisrael and would be destroyed. Binyamin saw that the ▓▓▓▓▓ was in Yosef's portion and would be destroyed. (Rashi, 45:14)

> Which fast days are connected to the חורבן הבית? Why was each Beit HaMikdash destroyed? How can we rectify the חורבן הבית?

נ* Yaakov blessed Pharaoh that the ▓▓▓▓▓ would have plenty of water. (Rashi, 47:10)

ס* The שטן tries to be harmful at a time when there is ▓▓▓▓▓ (Rashi, 44:29)

ע What did Yosef send his father?

פ Osnat was the daughter of ▓▓▓▓▓.

צ Yosef fell onto the ▓▓▓▓▓ of Binyamin.

ק* What was Yaakov reciting the first time he saw Yosef? (Rashi, 46:29)

> When and how many times a day is one obligated to say קריאת שמע? Explain the כוונה that is needed when reciting קריאת שמע and the way one should carefully articulate the words and letters of this prayer.

ר Yaakov took all of the ▓▓▓▓▓ that he had in Canaan and brought it with him down to Mitzrayim.

ש How many people came down with Yaakov to Mitzrayim?

ת Yosef told his brothers ▓▓▓▓▓ אל on the way back to Eretz Canaan. (45:24)

What did Pharaoh ask Yaakov when they met, and why? What was Yaakov's answer, and what can we learn from it?

Haftorah Highlights

פרשת ויגש concentrates on the reuniting of Yosef and his brothers. The *haftorah* describes the division between the Kingdom of Yehuda and the rest of Benei Yisrael. The *navi* Yechezkel instructs שבט יהודה and Benei Yisrael to unite through their common purpose of serving Hashem. (*Yechezkel* 37:15–28)

Learning Lesson

When Yosef revealed himself to his brothers, they were so ashamed of what they had done that they were unable to speak. Yosef comforted his brothers by encouraging them to come close and reminding them that he is their brother. Sometimes, we get angry with people for silly reasons. Yosef teaches us to be forgiving, especially to the people closest to us.

Parsha Points:

▶ Before Yaakov dies, he offers ברכות to Yosef's children, Efraim and Menashe. Yaakov offers ברכות to all of his children, and then he dies.

▶ Yosef and his brothers bury Yaakov in Eretz Canaan, with Avraham and Yitzchak, and they return to Mitzrayim.

▶ גלות מצרים, or the time that Benei Yisrael would be in Mitzrayim, begins.

Questions

א *    Yaakov wanted to tell his sons about ▓▓▓▓ ▓▓▓▓.

ב *    What is Yaakov's ברכה to Yosef?

ג    Who from שבט מנשה becomes a great leader of the Jewish people? (Rashi, 48:19)

ד    Which one of Yaakov's sons is compared to a snake?

ה    Which פסוק do we say every night before we go to sleep?

What is prohibited to do after קריאת שמע is recited before going to sleep? On which night of the year is one פטור from saying קריאת שמע על המיטה?

ו *    Which words indicated to Chazal that Yosef was not susceptible to an עין הרע?

ז *    ▓▓▓▓ was blessed before Yissachar even though he was younger. Why?

ח    Yissachar is compared to a ▓▓▓▓.

ט    Yaakov blessed Yissachar that his land would always be ▓▓▓▓.

י *    Yaakov placed his ▓▓▓▓ ▓▓▓▓ on Efraim's head because he saw that ▓▓▓▓ would come from שבט אפרים. (Rashi, 48:19)

כ *    What did the kings of Canaan hang on Yaakov's coffin when he died? (Rashi, 50:14)

ל * Which words in the parsha show that the מלכות would never leave שבט יהודה? (Rashi, 49:10)

מ How old was Yaakov when he died?

נ How does Yaakov tell his sons that he is leaving this world? (49:29)

ס Why didn't Yaakov want to be buried in Mitzrayim? (Rashi, 47:29)

ע Yosef made his brothers promise that they would remove his ▬▬▬▬ from Mitzrayim.

פ Yaakov reminded Yosef that when he came from ▬▬▬▬, Rachel died in Eretz Canaan.

צ * Yaakov blessed Yehuda that his land would be good for raising ▬▬▬▬. (Rashi, 49:12)

ק * Which רשע did Yaakov see would come from שבט לוי? (Rashi, 49:6)

ר When Yaakov blessed Yosef's children, he placed his hands on their ▬▬▬▬ just like we do today.

ש Which words in the parsha mean that Yaakov "switched his hands"?

ת * Yaakov gave ▬▬▬▬ to Shimon and Levi (Rashi, 49:7)

### Parsha Puzzler

Why does the parsha begin by telling us how long Yaakov lived? Why didn't Yaakov have all of his sons swear that they would bury him in Maarat HaMachpela, as opposed to only Yosef?

### Haftorah Highlights

As Yaakov approaches the end of his life, he offers his children blessings and advice to help them face the slavery in Mitzrayim. As David HaMelech approaches the end of his life, he prepares his son Shlomo to serve as a מלך ישראל. Although Yaakov and David were faced with different challenges, both insisted that their children should follow the ways of תורת ישראל. (*I Melachim* 2:1–12)

### Learning Lesson

Yaakov and Yosef demanded that they be buried in Eretz Yisrael. Even in the last moments of their lives, they showed that a Jewish person must always desire to return to his homeland, Eretz Yisrael.

ספר שמות

# SEFER SHEMOT

**Parsha Points:**

▷ Mitzrayim makes Benei Yisrael their slaves. Pharaoh persecutes Benei Yisrael and orders all of their newborn male children to be killed.

▷ Moshe is born to Yocheved and Amram. In order to save Moshe, Yocheved places him in a basket on the river. Pharaoh's daughter finds Moshe and brings him into her home.

▷ When Moshe grows older, he goes out to see Benei Yisrael in slavery. He kills an איש מצרי for striking a Jewish slave. Moshe flees from Pharaoh to Midyan.

▷ Moshe marries Yitro's daughter Tzippora in Midyan, and they have two sons.

▷ Moshe is a shepherd, and while tending his sheep in the desert, Hashem appears to him in a burning bush. Hashem appoints Moshe as the leader of Benei Yisrael. He instructs Moshe to confront Pharaoh, together with his brother Aharon, in order to take Benei Yisrael out of Mitzrayim.

▷ As messengers of Hashem, Moshe and Aharon perform two miracles in front of Pharaoh, but Pharaoh does not listen.

Questions

א   When Moshe got older, he went out to see the pain of Benei Yisrael, who were his ▓▓▓▓▓.

ב *  The מלאך המות wanted to kill Moshe because Moshe didn't give his son Eliezer a ▓▓▓▓▓. (Rashi, 4:24)

ג   Who was Moshe's elder son?

ד   Who were the two men who saw Moshe kill the איש מצרי? (Rashi, 2:13)

ה *  Pharaoh said ▓▓▓▓▓, which means he wanted to think of ways to destroy Benei Yisrael.

ו   When Hashem informs Moshe that he will confront Pharaoh, what was Moshe's response? (4:1)

ז   What was תיבת משה covered with?

ח   Yitro was Moshe's ▓▓▓▓▓ and Moshe was Yitro's ▓▓▓▓▓.

ט   Which word in the parsha shows that when Moshe was born the whole house had light? (Rashi, 2:2)

י   Who were Shifra and Pua? (Rashi, 1:15)

כ   Moshe said that he was ▓▓▓▓▓ ▓▓▓▓▓ ▓▓▓▓▓ ▓▓▓▓▓ and could not be a spokesperson for Hashem. (4:10)

ל   Which שבט was Moshe from?

מ   What was Miriam and Yocheved's job?

ג The מטה of Moshe turned into a ▨▨▨.

ס Hashem appeared to Moshe through the ▨▨▨.

ע Who was Moshe's father?

פ What did Moshe hide because he was afraid to look at Hashem? (3:6)

> Discuss the times during תפילה when we are supposed to close our eyes or keep them focused on the siddur, such as during ברכת כהנים, and שמונה עשרה, קריאת שמע. Why do we keep our eyes closed? How does it affect our כוונה?

צ What did Moshe's hand have on it when he took it out from his coat?

ק Moshe had to remove his shoes because the place where he stood was ▨▨▨.

> When else is it prohibited to have a partition between one's feet and the ground? How does this concept apply to *halacha* today?

ר Another name for Yitro was ▨▨▨.

ש How long did Yocheved hide Moshe before she put him in the תיבה? (2:2)

ת After Moshe challenged Pharaoh for the first time, Pharaoh forced Benei Yisrael to gather their own ▨▨▨.

## Parsha Puzzler

When Hashem told Moshe to approach Pharaoh and take Benei Yisrael out of Mitzrayim, Moshe said "הֵן לֹא יַאֲמִינוּ לִי." Why did Moshe assume that Benei Yisrael would not believe him? Why did Moshe hesitate to listen to Hashem's instructions?

## Haftorah Highlights

The parsha begins by describing the arrival of Klal Yisrael in Mitzrayim. This bitter slavery would mark the beginning of the Jewish nation. The *haftorah* begins by describing the reunification of Benei Yisrael and their redemption. Even though Benei Yisrael encounter גלות and hardships, such as the slavery in Mitzrayim, the *haftorah* comes to remind us that Hashem will always redeem the Jewish people. (*Yeshayahu* 27:6–28:13, 29:22–23 [*Yirmeyahu* 1:1–2:3])

## Learning Lesson

Yitro looked after Moshe and his family for many years and treated Moshe like his own son. Moshe was instructed by Hashem to go to Mitzrayim and confront Pharaoh. Out of respect, Moshe returned to Yitro's house to ask him permission to leave before he left to fulfill Hashem's commandment. Even when we are fulfilling the mitzvot of Hashem, it is important to be sensitive to people's feelings.

# ואראVA'ERA

## Parsha Points:

▸ Moshe warns Pharaoh that Hashem would send מכות upon Mitzrayim if he did not set Benei Yisrael free. The first plague that was sent, דם, transforms all of Mitzrayim's water into blood.

▸ After Pharaoh refuses to listen to Moshe, frogs are sent upon Mitzrayim. This plague is called צפרדע.

▸ As Pharaoh continues to refuse to set Benei Yisrael free, more מכות are sent, such as כינים – lice, ערוב – wild animals, דבר – pestilence that killed the animals, שכין – skin infections, and ברד – heavy hail.

## Questions

א  Who was Aharon's wife?

ב  The seventh מכה was ▨▨▨▨▨.

ג  Who were Levi's three sons?

ד *  Yocheved was Amram's ▨▨▨▨▨.

ה *  Which words in the פסוק demonstrate that Aharon and Moshe were equals? (Rashi, 6:26)

ו  What was Pharaoh's reaction after the ברד?

ז  What did Pharaoh allow Benei Yisrael to offer in the desert?

ח  Moshe hid the מצרי that he had killed in the ▨▨▨▨▨. Therefore, he was not allowed to bring מכת כינים upon the Mitzrim. (Rashi, 8:12)

> Discuss the concept of הכרת הטוב. Where else in the Torah do we find examples of הכרת הטוב?

ט  Which word in the parsha means "not yet"? (Rashi, 9:30)

י  Hashem promised to take Benei Yisrael out of Mitzrayim with His ▨▨▨▨▨.

כ  What was the third מכה?

ל  Hashem told Moshe that He would take Benei Yisrael ▨▨▨▨▨ ▨▨▨▨▨. (6:7)

מ * In this week's parsha, Eretz Yisrael is called a _____.

Discuss what a ירושה is. Differentiate between a ירושה and a מתנה. Why is Eretz Yisrael referred to as a ירושה?

נ * Who was Aharon's brother-in-law?

ס The suffering that Benei Yisrael experienced in Mitzrayim is referred to as מצרים _____.

ע Moshe needed Aharon to go with him to Pharaoh because he was an _____.

פ Who was Elazar's son and Aharon's grandson?

צ * The _____ taught us the importance of מסירות נפש.

Discuss examples throughout Jewish history of people who were מוסר נפש for Benei Yisrael. How does מסירות נפש exhibit itself today?

ק When Moshe told Benei Yisrael about יציאת מצרים, they did not listen to him because of _____ _____ _____ _____ (6:9).

ר Which three שבטים are mentioned in the parsha?

ש How old were Moshe and Aharon the first time they went to Pharaoh?

ת The frogs jumped into the _____ of Mitzrayim.

Did Hashem force Pharaoh to keep Benei Yisrael as slaves by hardening his heart? If so, how could Pharaoh have the freedom of choice to let Benei Yisrael go?

פרשת
וארא

demonstrates how Mitzrayim afflicted Benei Yisrael. In the *haftorah*, the *navi* Yechezkel also describes how Mitzrayim betrayed the Jewish people, because they did not help defend Benei Yisrael against Bavel. Although in the *haftorah* Mitzrayim does not persecute Benei Yisrael directly, their disregard for the welfare of Benei Yisrael results in Bavel's invasion of Eretz Yisrael and the destruction of the Beit HaMikdash. (*Yechezkel* 28:25–29:21)

The Torah says: הוא אהרן ומשה אשר אמר ה׳ להם הוציאו את בני ישראל מארץ מצרים (6:26). Rashi comments that Aharon and Moshe were equal. However, we know that Moshe was the greatest *navi*. Rav Moshe Feinstein explains that even though Moshe was a greater *navi*, Aharon tried to live up to his own full potential. For this reason, he was equated with Moshe. Hashem gives each one of us different strengths and talents, and we are expected to use them to their fullest potential.

**Parsha Points:**

▶ Moshe confronts Pharaoh and warns him of more מכות, but Pharaoh continues to refuse to let Benei Yisrael leave Mitzrayim.

▶ Hashem sends the מכות of ארבה – locusts, and חושך – darkness.

▶ Benei Yisrael are instructed to prepare their first קרבן פסח and place the blood of the lamb from the sacrifice on their doorposts.

▶ The final מכה is מכת בכורות, during which every firstborn throughout all of Mitzrayim was killed. Pharaoh allows Benei Yisrael to leave Mitzrayim.

Questions

א    What is the first מכה mentioned in the parsha?

ב    Moshe warned Pharaoh that the ▓▓▓▓▓ of everyone in Mitzrayim will be killed.

ג    Hashem told Benei Yisrael that a ▓▓▓▓▓ has a right to the Torah just like the rest of Benei Yisrael.

ד    What did Hashem see on the doorposts?

ה    How does the first mitzva given to Benei Yisrael in the parsha begin?

> How was קידוש החודש done in the time of the Beit HaMikdash? How do we remember קידוש החודש today? What are the twelve Hebrew months? What is the time frame for קידוש לבנה? What are the *halachot* of קידוש לבנה?

ו    A father is commanded to tell his children the story of יציאת מצרים because it says ▓▓▓▓▓.

ז    What is another name for the קרבן פסח?

ח    Which מכה lasted for three days?

ט    What did Benei Yisrael have to do to the אגודת אזוב? (12:22)

י    How does the Torah prohibit חמץ and שאור for the seven days of Pesach? לא ▓▓▓▓▓.

כ    One of the animals that can be used for the קרבן פסח is called a ▓▓▓▓▓.

ל    Hashem did מכת בכורות in the middle of the ▓▓▓▓▓.

מ   Benei Yisrael placed blood on the ████████, and this is why
    we have ████████ on our doorposts.

> What does a mezuza have inside of it? On which side of the
> doorpost do we hang the mezuza? What do some people
> do when they walk by a mezuza?

נ   The ████████ of the קרבן פסח must be burned in the morning.

ס *   The utensil which holds the blood from the קרבן פסח is called
    a ████████. (Rashi, 12:22)

ע   The ארבה ate all of the ████████ from the fields.

פ   Which mitzva is found at the end of the parsha? (13:2)

> Who has to have a פדיון הבן? How do we do a פדיון הבן, and
> on which day after the baby is born?

צ *   How does the קרבן פסח have to be cooked?

ק   The first mitzva that the Jewish people were commanded as a
    nation is called ████████.

ר   One of the four sons is a ████████. (Rashi, 13:18)

ש   For how many days is it prohibited to have חמץ in your house?

> What is חמץ? What is מכירת חמץ? What is בדיקת חמץ? What
> is ביעור חמץ?

ת   Who is not allowed to eat from the קרבן פסח? (12:45)

**Parsha Puzzler**

Why did Hashem take Benei Yisrael out of Mitzrayim בעצם היום, in the middle of the day? What else happened in the Torah בעצם היום?

**Haftorah Highlights**

From the beginning of the *haftorah*, Yirmeyahu describes the punishment and fate Mitzrayim will suffer at the hands of the Babylonian Empire. As in the *haftorah* of פרשת וארא, this can be compared to the plagues described in the parsha, where Pharaoh and the Mitzrim are defeated by Hashem and Klal Yisrael's redemption begins. (*Yirmeyahu* 46:13–28)

**Learning Lesson**

Benei Yisrael made מצה because they had to leave Mitzrayim in a hurry. מצות and מצוות are similar words. The *Mechilta* comments that just like מצות are baked quickly, so too should we show our eagerness to perform the מצוות without delay.

# בשלח
# BESHALACH

▸ Three days after Benei Yisrael leave Mitzrayim, Pharaoh and the Mitzrim pursue them.

▸ Benei Yisrael call to Moshe for help after they see the Mitzrim running after them from behind and the sea blocking them in front. Hashem instructs Moshe to tell Benei Yisrael to continue walking into the sea and have faith that Hashem will save them. Benei Yisrael continue, and the sea splits for them. When the Mitzrim follow Benei Yisrael into the sea, it closes on them. Benei Yisrael rejoice and sing to Hashem. This miracle is called קריעת ים סוף.

▸ As Benei Yisrael continue traveling, they were short of drinking water and they complain to Moshe. Hashem miraculously provides them with water to drink. Food is provided miraculously through the מן that fell from שמים.

▸ Amalek attacks Benei Yisrael, but they are defeated because of Benei Yisrael's belief in Hashem.

Questions

א   Which פסוק in the parsha is the beginning of a תפילה that we say every morning?

> In which part of תפילת שחרית is אז ישיר found? Why is אז ישיר part of פסוקי דזמרא? Discuss the *halachot* of פסוקי דזמרא. How does it begin? How does it end?

ב   When Benei Yisrael were in the ים סוף, they walked ▬▬▬▬. (14:22)

ג*   Which words in the parsha show that there is no limit to how much we can describe Hashem's greatness? (Rashi, 15:1)

ד*   When Benei Yisrael came out of Mitzrayim, Hashem would not let them travel ▬▬▬▬.

ה   Why did Moshe take Yosef's bones out of Mitzrayim? (13:19)

ו*   In the war with Amalek, when was Benei Yisrael stronger, and when was Amalek stronger (17:11)?

ז   What did the מן look like?

ח   Who was Miriam's son? (Rashi, 16:10)

ט   What was both under and on top of the מן?

י   Which direction is mentioned twice in the שירת הים?

כ   ▬▬▬▬ was married to Miriam.

ל   What do we use every Shabbat to remember the מן?

ב Who started to sing to Hashem after קריעת ים סוף?

ג Hashem told Moshe, "▨▨▨▨▨▨," and the water will cover the Mitzrim. (14:26)

ס On the first day that Benei Yisrael left Mitzrayim, they arrived in ▨▨▨▨▨. (Rashi, 13:20)

ע What did Hashem lead Benei Yisrael with during the day?

פ After קריעת ים סוף, all of the nations of the world had ▨▨▨▨▨ of Benei Yisrael.

צ The מן tasted like ▨▨▨▨▨.

ק Which miracle from the parsha do we refer to on the seventh day of Pesach? ▨▨▨▨▨ ▨▨▨▨▨ ▨▨▨▨▨.

ר Where were Benei Yisrael staying when they started to complain that they had no water?

ש What do we call the Shabbat when פרשת בשלח is read?

ת * What did Aharon and Chur do to Moshe's hands during the war with Amalek?

The Torah says that when Moshe's hands were raised, Benei Yisrael were stronger than Amalek. Why should this influence the victory of Benei Yisrael?

Haftorah Highlights

After קריעת ים סוף, Miriam leads Benei Yisrael in a song praising Hashem's greatness. The *haftorah* describes the war that Benei Yisrael had with the Pelishtim. Here Benei Yisrael are led to victory by Devora, and after the Pelishtim are defeated, Devora sings a song praising Hashem. (*Shoftim* 4:4–5:31)

Learning Lesson

The Gemara says that at קריעת ים סוף even the simplest person was able to see the greatness and miraculous nature of Hashem. Miracles happen every day. We have to be sensitive enough to focus on the world around us and appreciate the hand of Hashem in everything.

82 | The Family Parsha Book

# יתרו
# YITRO

▶ Yitro comes to join Benei Yisrael. He suggests to Moshe to gather a group of wise men to help him.

▶ Benei Yisrael receive the Torah at Har Sinai.

Questions

א What is the first commandment of the עשרת הדברות?

ב * What are the Jewish women called in the parsha, and why? (Rashi, 19:3)

> What type of mitzvot are women obligated in, and why?

ג It is prohibited to build a מזבח ⬚⬚⬚⬚⬚. (20:22)

ד * Moshe was the ⬚⬚⬚⬚⬚ for Benei Yisrael from morning until the night. (Rashi, 18:13)

ה Benei Yisrael waited by the ⬚⬚⬚⬚⬚ to receive the Torah. (19:2)

ו * How do we know that Benei Yisrael united in order to receive the Torah? (Rashi, 19:2)

> Discuss the importance of אחדות among Benei Yisrael. Where else in תנ"ך do we see אחדות? When did Benei Yisrael split, and what were the consequences? How can we better encourage אחדות among Benei Yisrael?

ז What is the fourth commandment of the עשרת הדברות?

> List various mitzvot of Shabbat. Differentiate between מצוות דאורייתא, מצוות דרבנן, and the concept of רוח שבת.

ח When the Torah was given, the sound of the שופר was ⬚⬚⬚⬚⬚.

ט In order to receive the Torah, Benei Yisrael had to make sure to remain ⬚⬚⬚⬚⬚.

י Who heard about מלחמת עמלק and קריעת ים סוף? (Rashi, 18:1)

כ What is the fifth commandment of the עשרת הדברות?

How does one fulfill the mitzva of כיבוד אב ואם? Why is it so difficult to fulfill this mitzva? Give examples of ways we can perform this mitzva in our own homes.

ל What are the last five commandments of the עשרת הדברות?

מ Hashem told Moshe that Benei Yisrael should be a ▓▓▓▓▓ ▓▓▓▓▓. (19:6)

נ How did Benei Yisrael respond when they were given the commandments?

ס Benei Yisrael received the Torah in ▓▓▓▓▓ מדבר.

ע What was on the top of the mountain when the Torah was given?

פ Another name for Yitro is ▓▓▓▓▓. (Rashi, 18:1)

צ Whom did Yitro take with him to greet Moshe?

ק* On Shabbat, the מן did not fall because it was a ▓▓▓▓▓ יום. (Rashi, 20:11)

ר Moshe appointed great men to be the ▓▓▓▓▓ of Benei Yisrael. (18:25)

ש What did Benei Yisrael have to wash before מתן תורה?

ת* Yitro was also called חובב because it means to love, and Yitro loved the ▓▓▓▓▓. (Rashi, 18:1)

Why was the commandment to keep Shabbat given before the commandment of כיבוד אב ואם?

Haftorah Highlights

Benei Yisrael received the Torah and were described in the parsha as a גוי קדוש. In the *haftorah*, Yeshayahu says that he too was privileged to see the קדושה of Hashem in the Mikdash from where the מלאכים would call to each other, "קדוש קדוש קדוש ה' צבאות מלא כל הארץ כבודו." Yeshayahu encouraged Benei Yisrael to return to the ways of Hashem by living a life of קדושה. (*Yeshayahu* 6:1–7:6, 9:5–6)

Learning Lesson

Yitro advised Moshe to gather seventy זקנים to help him rule Benei Yisrael. Moshe immediately accepted Yitro's advice. Even though Moshe was the greatest leader of the Jewish people, he was open to new ideas that would help Benei Yisrael. It is important to listen to advice and include ideas that can be helpful to us as well as to others.

# משפטים
# MISHPATIM

Parsha Points:

▶ The parsha lists many important mitzvot, both בין אדם למקום –
between man and Hashem, and בין אדם לחברו – between man
and his fellow man.

Questions

א   What is a female servant called?

ב   ▨▨▨▨ are brought to the ▨▨▨▨ on Shavuot.

> What are the שבעת המינים and which ברכה אחרונה do you say on them? If you are about to eat all of the שבעת המינים, in which order should you make the ברכה ראשונה, and which should you eat first?

ג   This person should not be taken advantage of and must be treated kindly.

ד   Against which item does the master pierce his servant's ear?

ה   ▨▨▨▨ ▨▨▨▨ is the mitzva to return lost items to their owner.

> Explain which items must be returned and which items you can keep if you find them, and why.

ו*   How does the parsha begin, and why? (Rashi, 21:1)

ז, ח*   Two acts that you are not allowed to do during the שמיטה year are ▨▨▨▨ and ▨▨▨▨. (Rashi, 23:11)

> Explain the concept of שמיטה. Why do we keep שמיטה? How do we keep it today?

ט   An animal that dies is called a ▨▨▨▨. (22:12)

י   The Torah says that we have to be careful not to tease or hurt the feelings of a ▨▨▨▨.

כ What does a person have to pay if he damages someone's property?

ל What words tell us that we are not allowed to eat meat and milk together?

> Which things do we have in the kitchen to separate meat and milk? How long do we have to wait between eating meat and milk? What do we have to do after eating milk in order to eat meat?

מ How do we know that one is not allowed to lie?

נ Who were the two sons of Aharon that went up with Moshe to Har Sinai?

ס What is done to an ox that kills someone?

ע An ▇▇▇▇▇ ▇▇▇▇▇ works for his master six years and is freed in the seventh year.

פ One of the boundaries of Eretz Yisrael is from the ים סוף to the ▇▇▇▇ ים. (23:31)

צ בית דין has to be careful not to punish a ▇▇▇▇.

ק Shavuot is also called ▇▇▇▇ חג ה.

ר Which words tell us that if you hurt someone you have to pay for his or her medical bills?

ש From which fruits can one bring the ביכורים?

ת * Which words in the parsha show that Moshe had to clarify all of the *halachot* in the Torah for Benei Yisrael? (Rashi, 21:1)

## Parsha Puzzler

Which kind of mitzvot are called משפטים? What are other types of mitzvot called, and why? List examples.

## Haftorah Highlights

The parsha begins by introducing the mitzva of עבד עברי and how he is set free on the שמיטה year. The *haftorah* begins by telling us that King Tzidkiyahu freed the עבדים עבריים, but in the end, the wealthy people took control of their עבדים again. This was a terrible sin, and it resulted in the fall of King Tzidkiyahu and the Kingdom of Israel. The *haftorah* ends as Hashem assures Benei Yisrael that His ברית with them will last. (*Yirmeyahu* 34:8–22, 33:25–26)

## Learning Lesson

פרשת משפטים is concerned with respecting people's belongings. השבת אבידה teaches us to return things that we find to their owner. The laws of נזק teach us to take responsibility if we hurt people or damage their property. The Torah instructs us to be sensitive to people's feelings and respect their property just as we respect ourselves and our own property.

# תרומה
# TERUMA

### Parsha Points:

▸ The Torah instructs Benei Yisrael how to build the Mishkan. The Mishkan traveled with Benei Yisrael in the מדבר, and it was the place where they offered sacrifices and demonstrated their commitment to Hashem.

▸ The Torah instructs Benei Yisrael how to make the כלי המשכן, the utensils used to serve Hashem in the Mishkan. Some of these include the ארון, the כפורת which covered the ארון, the כרובים which sat on top of the ארון, the שלחן, the מנורה, and the מזבח העולה.

**Questions**

א   Which stones were placed on the אפוד and the חושן?

ב   What was one of the ingredients of the שמן המשחה?

ג   There were three ▨▨▨▨ on one side of the מנורה and another three ▨▨▨▨ on the other side. (25:33)

ד   What did Hashem do from on top of the כפורת between the כרובים? (25:22)

ה*   תרומה means ▨▨▨▨. (Rashi, 25:2)

> What are the different ways to give צדקה, and what is the most preferred way?

ו   The ▨▨▨▨ ▨▨▨▨ were the hooks on the pillars of the Mishkan.

ז   What covered the table in the Mishkan?

ח   תכלת is made from the blood of a ▨▨▨▨.

ט   The ▨▨▨▨ were on the corners of the ארון and made of gold.

י   What is the name of the panels that the Mishkan was made out of? (26:1)

כ   Which two figures sat on top of the ארון?

ל   ▨▨▨▨ were loops that helped hold the curtains.

מ   Hashem showed Moshe the form of the ▨▨▨▨ before Benei Yisrael built it.

נ What covered the מזבח העולה?

ס The wings of the כרובים were ________ on top of the כפורת.

ע What was the inner layer of the ארון made out of?

פ What are the corners of the ארון called? (25:12)

צ * In which direction was the שלחן placed in the Mishkan?

ק Wooden planks used in the Mishkan are called ________. (26:15)

ר What was the shape of the מזבח?

ש * ________ ________ ________ was used to make the נר תמיד burn in the Mishkan. (Rashi, 25:6)

ת * Which animal was created in order to use its skin for the מזבח? (Rashi, 25:5)

The Torah says ועשו לי מקדש ושכנתי בתוכם – "And you shall make for Me a Mikdash, and I will dwell among them." The Torah should have said ושכנתי בתוכו, "and I will dwell in it," instead of בתוכם. Why is this commandment written in the plural?

The parsha describes the construction of the Mishkan and the *haftorah* describes King Shlomo's construction of the Beit HaMikdash. (*I Melachim* 5:26–6:13)

The Torah describes every detail with regard to building the Mishkan. Regarding קדושה, one should pay attention to all aspects of mitzvot, and attempt to derive spiritual inspiration in the different forms and ways the Torah makes it available.

**Parsha Points:**

▶ In order to serve in the Mishkan, the Kohanim had to wear special clothing called בגדי כהונה. The Torah explains how to make the various clothing worn by the Kohen Gadol and the Kohen Hedyot.

▶ Some of the בגדים worn by the Kohen Gadol were the חושן משפט – the breastplate, the אפוד – like an apron, the מעיל – cloak, and the ציץ – headplate. All Kohanim wore מכנסיים – pants, כתונת – a shirt, אבנט – a belt, and a מגבעת – a hat.

א  One of the colors of the חושן משפט was ▮▮▮▮▮▮.

ב *  Part of dedicating the מזבח was to bring a קרבן תמיד in the ▮▮▮▮▮▮ and another one ▮▮▮▮▮▮.

ג  What did the מזבח for the קטורת have that the מזבח העולה did not have? (Rashi, 30:3)

ד  The Kohen took ▮▮▮▮▮▮ and sprinkled it on the מזבח.

ה  Which type of Kohen had only four garments to wear? (Rashi, 28:42)

ו  What is the first word of the parsha, and whom is it referring to?

ז  It is prohibited to offer a ▮▮▮▮▮▮ קטורת on the מזבח. (30:9)

ח  What kind of work had to be done in order to prepare the stones for the חושן? (28:11)

ט  There were four ▮▮▮▮▮▮ of stones on the חושן משפט.

י  The ▮▮▮▮▮▮ of Aharon and the ▮▮▮▮▮▮ of his sons are inaugurated by being anointed Kohanim. (Rashi, 29:9)

כ  What were the shoulder straps attached to the אפוד called? (28:27)

ל  Where were the אורים ותומים placed on Aharon? (28:30)

מ  Aharon wore a long cloak which was called a ▮▮▮▮▮▮. (29:31)

נ  What is another name for the ציץ? (Rashi, 29:6)

ס    What did Aharon and his sons do to an animal before it was brought as a קרבן?

ע    One of the קרבנות that had to be brought every day was called ▆▆▆▆▆▆. (29:42)

פ    What were connected to the bottom of the מעיל?

צ    This בגד was worn by the Kohen on his forehead.

ק    Every morning Aharon burned the ▆▆▆▆▆ on the מזבח הזהב.

ר    Which words describing a certain smell demonstrate that the קרבן was accepted?

ש    How many garments did a Kohen Gadol wear? (28:42)

ת    The lamp that held the candle in the Mishkan had to be readied ▆▆▆▆▆▆.

## Parsha Puzzler

Each one of the garments worn by the Kohen Gadol helped Benei Yisrael be forgiven for a different sin. Which sin did each garment atone for?

## Haftorah Highlights

In פרשת תצוה, Hashem tells the Kohanim how to sanctify themselves and the מזבח for His עבודה. In the *haftorah*, Hashem shows the *navi* Yechezkel how Benei Yisrael will sanctify the third Beit HaMikdash and offer קרבנות. This קדושה will remain because of Benei Yisrael's dedication and commitment to Hashem. (*Yechezkel 43:10–27*)

## Learning Lesson

The חושן משפט, which was placed on the chest of the Kohen Gadol and close to his heart, had twelve different stones on it. Each stone represented a שבט of Benei Yisrael. This way, when the Kohen did the עבודה in the Mishkan, he had each שבט in mind. It is important to remember that while all people are different, we share the same Torah. We should see past our differences and concentrate on what unites us as one.

# כי תישא

# KI TISA

▷ Moshe goes up to Har Sinai to receive the לוחות הברית that had the עשרת הדברות on them.

▷ While Moshe is on Har Sinai, Benei Yisrael rebel against Hashem by building and worshiping an עגל זהב. This sin is known as חטא העגל. When Moshe descends from Har Sinai, he breaks the לוחות הברית after he sees Benei Yisrael sinning. שבט לוי kill the people who worshiped the עגל. Hashem threatens to destroy Benei Yisrael, but Moshe prays on their behalf and appeases Hashem's anger.

▷ All men over the age of twenty from Benei Yisrael are counted by bringing the מחצית השקל, a half-shekel, to Moshe. The money was used for the עבודה in the Mishkan.

Questions

א    Shabbat is an ▒▒▒▒▒ between Hashem and Benei Yisrael.

> What are some of the things we do on Shabbat to show that it is a special day between Benei Yisrael and Hashem? What are some of the things we avoid doing on Shabbat to preserve its קדושה?

ב    Who helped Moshe build the כלים for the Mishkan because he was given wisdom from Hashem?

ג    After he saw the עגל הזהב, Moshe told Benei Yisrael that they did a חטא ▒▒▒▒▒. (32:30)

ד    Even a ▒▒▒▒▒ has to give the מחצית השקל.

ה    What did Moshe ask from Hashem in the parsha? (33:18)

ו*    Which מידה of Hashem teaches us that He punishes with רחמנות? (Rashi, 34:7)

ז*    On which date did Moshe go up to the שמים to get the Torah for the first time? (Rashi, 32:1)

ח    Benei Yisrael worshiped an idol while Moshe went up to get the Torah. This sin is called ▒▒▒▒▒ ▒▒▒▒▒.

ט    The קטורת had to be ▒▒▒▒▒. (30:35)

י*    Which fast day is the day the לוחות were broken?

כ    This כלי in the Mishkan was made out of copper.

ל    Which שבט did not sin in the חטא העגל?

מ    What was Moshe's cry to Benei Yisrael after he saw the עגל הזהב, and who else used this same cry (32:26)?

נ    Benei Yisrael used ▓▓▓▓▓▓, which belonged to the ▓▓▓▓▓▓, to make the עגל הזהב.

ס    How does Hashem tell Moshe that Benei Yisrael rebelled against Him? (32:8)

ע    Hashem refers to Benei Yisrael as an ▓▓▓▓▓▓.

פ    How did Hashem speak to Moshe?

צ *    What is another word in the parsha that means Benei Yisrael sinned? (Rashi, 32:6)

ק    Moshe had to cover his face with a mask because his face had ▓▓▓▓▓▓ ▓▓▓▓▓▓.

ר    One of the thirteen מדות of Hashem that shows that He is merciful.

ש    How many times a year is a person obligated to come to the Beit HaMikdash with קרבנות?

ת    The מחצית השקל was a ▓▓▓▓▓▓ to the Mishkan.

**Parsha Puzzler**

Why should everyone have to give the same amount of money for the Mishkan (מחצית השקל)? If a rich person wants to give more money, why can't he? After all, it is צדקה.

**Haftorah Highlights**

The incident of חטא העגל was the first time Benei Yisrael worshiped עבודה זרה as a nation. After חטא העגל, Benei Yisrael had to do תשובה and return to Hashem. In the *haftorah*, Benei Yisrael are once again swayed to worship עבודה זרה under the leadership of the wicked King Achav. The *navi* Eliyahu challenges Achav and נביאי הבעל, exposes their falseness, and encourages Benei Yisrael to return to Hashem. The *haftorah* ends as all of Benei Yisrael say "ה' הוא האלקים." (*I Melachim* 18:1–39)

**Learning Lesson**

The חטא העגל occurred right after Benei Yisrael received the Torah at Har Sinai. The Gemara says that Benei Yisrael went מאיגרא רמא לבירא עמיקתא, "from the highest level to the lowest level." Even though Benei Yisrael had experienced מתן תורה, they still gave in to their יצר הרע and committed a terrible sin. We have to be careful not to grow overly confident in ourselves. We must always look for new learning experiences that will help us achieve greater spirituality to preserve our relationship with Hashem.

ויקהל

# ויקהל
# VAYAK'HEL

**Parsha Points:**

▶ Moshe reminds Benei Yisrael of the mitzva of Shabbat, and then he reviews the construction of the Mishkan and the כלי המשכן.

▶ Moshe informs Benei Yisrael that Betzalel is in charge of constructing the כלי המשכן.

Questions

א   Who from שבט דן worked on building the Mishkan? (Rashi, 35:34)

ב   Who from שבט יהודה worked on building the Mishkan?

ג   What are the cups that hold the oil on the מנורה called?

ד *  Moshe used his ▓▓▓▓▓ in order to gather the people. (Rashi, 35:1)

ה *  Moshe gathered Benei Yisrael when he came down from the ▓▓▓▓▓ on the day after ▓▓▓▓▓ יום. (Rashi, 35:1)

ו   ▓▓▓▓▓ days Benei Yisrael do מלאכה and on the seventh day is Shabbat.

ז   What were the beams, rings, and bars of the Mishkan covered with?

ח   Which type of person was called upon by Moshe to help build the Mishkan? (36:2)

ט   Which מלאכה did the women do specially for the Mishkan?

י   The shovels used in the Mishkan are called ▓▓▓▓▓.

כ   This precious metal was donated by Benei Yisrael to help make the כלים.

ל   Which מלאכה of Shabbat is specified in the parsha?

מ   The women dedicated their ▓▓▓▓▓ for building the כיור.

נ   Moshe expected the ▓▓▓▓▓ to give תרומות for the Mishkan. (35:5)

ס   A gold embroidery was לשלחן ▓▓▓▓▓.

ע   What are Benei Yisrael called at the beginning of the parsha?

פ   The מנורה was decorated with ▓▓▓▓▓. (37:17)

צ   Rings were placed on the two ▓▓▓▓▓ and the two ▓▓▓▓▓ of the מזבח in order to carry it. (37:27)

ק   Which word in the parsha means corner?

ר   A person who makes perfumed oils is called a ▓▓▓▓▓, and a person who creates beautiful materials is called a ▓▓▓▓▓. (37:29, 38:18)

ש   What are the two oils that were made for the Mishkan called? (35:28)

ת   The beautiful color used on the screens of the Mishkan that is also used for tzitzit is called ▓▓▓▓▓.

**Parsha Puzzler**

Why does the Torah repeat the construction of the Mishkan and its כלים after it was already written in פרשת תרומה?

**Haftorah Highlights**

פרשת ויקהל describes the intricate details and skills needed to finish the כלי המשכן and the Mishkan itself. The *haftorah* follows by describing the skilled craftsmen that King Shlomo recruited from King Chiram of Tzur for building the Beit HaMikdash and crafting the כלי המקדש. (*I Melachim* 7:40–50 [*I Melachim* 7:13–26])

**Learning Lesson**

The Torah introduces the seventh day – Shabbat – by first mentioning the six weekdays of work. Many explain that this reminds us that all of the days of the week revolve around the holiest day, Shabbat. Our job is to try and sanctify everything in this world for a greater purpose and to recognize that there is קדושה in everything.

# פקודי
# PEKUDEI

Parsha Points:

▶ The walls and structure of the Mishkan are built. The Torah records the measurements of the Mishkan, including the height and width of the walls and the length of the wooden beams and poles.

▶ The Mishkan is covered with skins called עורות. They are made of different materials.

▶ The construction of the Mishkan is completed.

*Questions*

א   Who was the person in charge of appointing jobs for each family in שבט לוי?

ב   Where in the Mishkan was the כיור located?

ג   What are the edges of the חושן משפט called? (39:15)

ד *   The ציץ was attached to the מצנפת using ▭▭▭▭. (Rashi, 39:31)

ה   All of the gold and silver used for the Mishkan was counted according to the ▭▭▭▭ שקל.

ו *   What was one of the ברכות that Moshe gave to Benei Yisrael after they completed the work for the Mishkan? (Rashi, 39:43)

ז   Name a measurement used for the חושן. (39:9)

ח   What was the type of artwork used to create the אפוד? (39:3)

ט   When the כלים were completed and brought to Moshe, only the מנורה was called ▭▭▭▭. (39:37)

י   The כיור was used to wash the Kohanim's ▭▭▭▭.

> Discuss the basis for נטילת ידיים and the concept of סרך תרומה. When do we wash the hands of the Kohanim today, and why? How much of the Kohanim's hands needs to be washed?

כ *   The beginning of the parsha talks about counting the ▭▭▭▭ of the Mishkan. (Rashi, 38:21)

ל   What is prohibited to do to the מעיל? (39:23)

מ *   Which word appears twice in one פסוק at the beginning of the parsha, and why? (Rashi, 38:21)

נ   In which position was the מנורה placed in the Mishkan?

ס   How does the Torah command that the פרוכת should be a screen for the ארון? (40:3)

ע   Benei Yisrael would travel when the _____ was raised by Hashem from upon the Mishkan.

פ   What type of writing was used on the אבני שוהם? (39:6)

צ   Which בגד was worn on top of the מצנפת like a crown? (39:30)

ק   When the מזבח is sanctified it is called _____.

ר   What was the מעיל decorated with?

ש   _____ were chains that held the אפוד.

ת   One of the covers for the Mishkan was made from the skins of the _____. (39:34)

**Parsha Puzzler**

The Torah shows us how to live our lives. Why, then, does it have to give us such a detailed account of every material used for the מלאכת המשכן? Is it necessary for us to know the exact number of nails used to support the Mishkan?

**Haftorah Highlights**

The *haftorah* describes the completion of the Beit HaMikdash. King Shlomo dedicates the Beit HaMikdash to Hashem just like Benei Yisrael completed the construction of the Mishkan in the מדבר. (*I Melachim* 7:51–8:21 [*I Melachim* 7:40–50])

**Learning Lesson**

The Gemara in Tractate Berachot says that Moshe was going to make the כלי המשכן and then build the Mishkan itself. Betzalel told Moshe that they should first build the Mishkan, and then fill it with the כלים. Moshe listened to Betzalel, demonstrating his modesty and eagerness to learn from everyone. It is important to listen to and learn from people.

ספר ויקרא

# SEFER VAYIKRA

# ויקרא
# VAYIKRA

Parsha Points:

▶ The Torah describes different קרבנות. A קרבן חטאת and קרבן אשם are offered to atone for sins. A קרבן עולה is offered as a gift to Hashem. A קרבן תודה is offered when someone wants to thank Hashem for something good that happened to him.

▶ There are also קרבנות that are offered as part of serving Hashem regularly in the Mishkan. The קרבן תמיד was offered twice every day, and the קרבן מוסף was offered on Shabbat, Rosh Chodesh, and Yom Tov.

▶ Some of the processes in preparing a קרבן include סמיכה – placing the hands on the animal, וידוי – confession of sins, שחיטה – slaughtering the animal, קבלה – collecting the blood, זריקה – sprinkling the blood, and הקטרה – placing the animal on the מזבח.

▶ Birds can also be offered as קרבנות instead of animals. Some of the processes in preparing a bird as an offering include מליקה – slaughtering the bird, and מיצוי – draining its blood onto the side of the מזבח.

▶ A poor person who cannot afford an animal or bird as an offering can offer a קרבן מנחה. This קרבן is a cake, and some of its ingredients include flour, water, and oil.

▶ Other, less common קרבנות are also described in the parsha, such as the קרבן חטאת that is brought if an entire community sins.

Questions

א    Which word in the parsha teaches us that one cannot offer
קרבנות that are stolen? (Rashi, 1:2)

ב *    This word confirms that one must bring an animal and not a
beast for a sacrifice. (Rashi, 1:2)

ג    Which is the part of an animal that must be removed before
it is offered as a קרבן?

> Discuss which parts of an animal are prohibited to eat.

ד    What did the Kohen sprinkle on the side of the מזבח?

ה    What is the process of skinning the animal for a קרבן called?
(1:6)

ו *    Which words in the parsha tell us that if someone stole
something they have to bring a קרבן and return what they stole?
(5:23)

ז    The Kohen takes the blood of the קרבן עולה and does ▭.

ח    What kind of קרבן does a person bring for doing a sin by
mistake?

> What do we do today instead of offering קרבנות? Which part
> of the שמונה עשרה demonstrates our desire to offer קרבנות
> again?

ט    A קרבן אשם is offered if someone touches things that are
▭ and does not know. (5:2)

י    If a person cannot afford to bring a sheep or goat for the קרבן
אשם, he can bring two ▭ instead.

כ In a קרבן שלמים, which organ in the animal is removed and burned on the מזבח? (3:4)

ל * ויקרא אל משה: this is a ______ and a ______. (Rashi, 1:1)

מ * From where in the אהל מועד did Hashem speak to Moshe? (Rashi, 1:1)

נ * Which word is used only with regard to a קרבן מנחה, and why? (Rashi, 2:1)

ס The Kohen places his hands on the head of an animal before he offers it as a קרבן. What is this called?

ע Which קרבן מנחה is brought from barley?

פ How does a קרבן מנחה על המחבת have to be offered? (2:6)

צ This is a type of animal acceptable to be offered as a קרבן: ______.

ק All קרבנות which must be eaten by Kohanim in the Mikdash are called ______.

ר After the קרבנות are burned on the מזבח, they create a ______ for Hashem.

ש How many times does the Kohen do זריקת הדם on the מזבח?

ת An animal can be offered as a קרבן only if it is ______.

**Parsha Puzzler**

Hashem does not need food. Why do we offer קרבנות to Him?

**Haftorah Highlights**

פרשת ויקרא deals with קרבנות. People give קרבנות to show their devotion to Hashem. In the *haftorah*, the *navi* Yeshayahu criticizes Benei Yisrael because they did not offer קרבנות and did not take advantage of the opportunity to get close to Hashem. Many people began to worship עבודה זרה. Yeshayahu encourages Benei Yisrael to do תשובה and worship Hashem. (*Yeshayahu* 43:21–44:23)

**Learning Lesson**

Anyone who could not afford to offer an animal as a קרבן could bring a modest קרבן מנחה instead. Everyone was given the opportunity to bring a קרבן. Hashem is not impressed by a person's wealth, but rather by a person's sincerity and desire to serve Him. We too should not be impressed by what a person has, but by how they devote themselves to Hashem.

# צו
# TZAV

**Parsha Points:**

▶ The Torah describes the different kinds of קרבן אשם. An אשם מעילות is offered if a person derived benefit from הקדש, something designated for the Mishkan. An אשם תלוי is offered if a person is unsure whether he has committed a sin or not. An אשם גזילות is offered if a person uses someone's property without permission.

▶ The parsha describes the *halachot* and circumstances under which one would offer a קרבן שלמים. A קרבן שלמים is offered when a person wants to thank Hashem for something, or if someone promises to bring a קרבן but has not specified what type of קרבן to bring.

▶ In this parsha, the Torah introduces for the first time the prohibition against eating the blood or fat of an animal that was sacrificed.

**Questions**

א  What had to be constantly on the מזבח?

ב  What time of day does the Kohen place wood on the מזבח?

> Which תפילה is related to the עבודה offered by the Kohanim in the morning? Discuss the *halachot* of שחרית. What is the time frame of תפילת שחרית?

ג *  Seven days before Yom Kippur, the כהן ▭▭▭▭ has to stay in the Beit HaMikdash to prepare. (Rashi, 8:34)

ד *  Why does the Kohen have to change his clothing before he cleans the מזבח? (Rashi, 6:4)

> Define דרך ארץ. How does דרך ארץ apply to our daily lives?

ה  What was Moshe told to do to Benei Yisrael before he anointed Aharon as the Kohen Gadol? (8:3)

ו  These words teach us that Aharon and his sons did everything that Hashem said without delay. (Rashi, 8:36)

ז  פרשת צו teaches us that we should do mitzvot with ▭▭▭▭. (Rashi, 6:2)

> Discuss the concept of זריזין מקדימין and how it applies to us.

ח  Which fatty part of the animal is it אסור to eat?

ט  When the ashes were cleaned off of the מזבח, they were brought to a place that was ▭▭▭▭.

י  Which thigh was given to the Kohen from a קרבן שלמים?

כ  What is the punishment for someone who eats from the קרבן שלמים when he is טמא?

ל  The basket of מצות used to inaugurate Aharon and his sons was kept ▬▬▬▬▬.

מ  The קרבן מנחה was offered on a ▬▬▬▬▬.

נ  What were the leftovers from the קרבנות called?

ס  Name one of the ingredients always included in the קרבן מנחת חביתין.

ע  How does the Torah instruct the Kohen to prepare the מזבח for the קרבן עולה? (6:5)

פ  A person is not allowed to eat a קרבן שלמים for more than a certain amount of days. What is the prohibition called if he even thinks about doing so?

צ  The gold band placed on the מצנפת around the head of the כהן is called the ▬▬▬▬▬.

ק  What is the process called when the Kohen measures the flour for the קרבן מנחה with his fingers?

ר  One of the breads that is covered in oil and brought with a קרבן שלמים is called ▬▬▬▬▬.

ש  For how many days can a person eat the קרבן שלמים before he has to burn the leftovers?

ת  What kind of קרבן does someone have to bring if they escape a dangerous situation?

What ברכה should a person say if he is saved miraculously? When should he say the ברכה?

**Parsha Puzzler**

What are the differences between a קרבן עולה and a קרבן שלמים? When and why is each one offered?

**Haftorah Highlights**

פרשת צו continues describing the *halachot* of the קרבנות. In the *haftorah*, the *navi* Yirmeyahu rebukes Benei Yisrael for bringing sacrifices to עבודה זרה. Yirmeyahu reminds Benei Yisrael that they must build a relationship with Hashem by practicing kindness and righteousness. (*Yirmeyahu* 7:21–8:3, 9:22–23)

**Learning Lesson**

It was prohibited for the קרבן מנחה to become חמץ, dough that rises slowly. The prohibition of חמץ in a מקום קדוש teaches us that we cannot approach קדושה slowly and wait for mitzvot to come to us. We have to serve Hashem by looking for opportunities to perform mitzvot without delay.

# שמיני
# SHMINI

**Parsha Points:**

▶ Benei Yisrael complete the construction of the Mishkan and offer קרבנות to Hashem for the dedication.

▶ Nadav and Avihu, two of Aharon's sons, offer קטורת in the Mishkan without receiving a sign from Hashem. As a result, they are killed.

▶ The Torah distinguishes between kosher and non-kosher animals and fish, and then lists the kosher and non-kosher birds.

## Questions

א  Who was called upon by Moshe on the eighth day of their inauguration of the Mishkan? (Rashi, 9:1)

ב  The קרבן מנחה that was offered by Aharon, his sons, and Benei Yisrael was ▇▇▇▇. (9:4)

ג  Which animal chews its cud but does not have split hooves?

> Ask for more examples of non-kosher animals, and discuss why they are not kosher.

ד  Name two types of birds that are אסור to eat.

> What kind of bird as a rule is not kosher, and why?

ה *  What was one of the reasons why Nadav and Avihu were killed? (Rashi, 10:2)

ו *  Which words in the parsha teach us that just like Hashem is holy, we must make our world holy? (Rashi, 11:44)

ז  What kind of fire did Nadav and Avihu offer on the מזבח?

ח  A dead insect can cause a כלי made of ▇▇▇▇ to become טמא if the insect falls inside of it.

ט  The parsha lists animals that are ▇▇▇▇ and animals that are ▇▇▇▇.

י  What is prohibited for the Kohanim to drink before they enter the אהל מועד?

Discuss when it is prohibited today to drink wine and when it is a mitzva?

ב Why are Benei Yisrael expected to be קדוש? (11:44, 45)

ל Why is it prohibited for the Kohanim to drink יין and שכר before they come to the אהל מועד? (10:10)

מ Give one sign of a kosher animal.

נ If someone is ▨▨▨▨ the ▨▨▨▨ of an animal, he becomes טמא. (11:36)

ס Name one of the requirements that a fish needs in order to be kosher.

ע If someone touches a dead animal, he becomes טמא until the ▨▨▨▨. (11:27)

פ During the time that the שמן משחה was on the Kohanim, it was prohibited for them to leave the ▨▨▨▨.

צ Give an example of a שרץ עוף. (Rashi, 11:20)

ק What is the second requirement that a fish needs in order to be kosher?

Ask for more examples of non-kosher fish, and discuss why they are not kosher.

ר Which day of the month was the *yom hashemini lamiluim*?

ש What is the second sign of a kosher animal?

ת What was prohibited for Kohanim to do to their hair and clothing when they entered the אהל מועד? (10:6)

**Parsha Puzzler**

The חזיר is the only animal that the Torah says is מפריס פרסה but not שוסעת שסע. Why does the Torah choose to describe the features of the pig exclusively?

**Haftorah Highlights**

פרשת שמיני marks the dedication of the Mishkan. The Torah says that with this dedication, Benei Yisrael escorted the שכינה into the Mishkan. The *haftorah* describes how King David escorted the ארון קדש to Yerushalayim. This was done with joy and celebration as Benei Yisrael welcomed the שכינה into Yerushalayim. (*II Shmuel 6:1–7:17*)

**Learning Lesson**

Nadav and Avihu had good intentions when they brought their offering to Hashem in the Mishkan, but they were punished. Chazal explain that this was because they did not consult with Moshe and Aharon to see if their offering was appropriate at that particular time. Even when our intentions are good, it is important to consult with others and consider their advice.

# תזריע מצורע
# TAZRIA METZORA

▶ The Torah talks about a מצורע, someone who has צרעת. A מצורע is טמא, and he must remain outside the Machane Yisrael, the camp of Benei Yisrael. There is a process that the מצורע must follow in order to purify himself and once again be part of the Machane Yisrael.

▶ צרעת can also afflict houses and clothing, and the Torah describes how to purify them as well.

א The beginning of the parsha talks about an ▬▬▬▬ who gives birth.

ב What is one type of bird that a woman offers as a קרבן after she has given birth?

ג Someone whose hair falls out is called a ▬▬▬▬, and he is טהור. (13:41)

ד What is a poor person called in the Torah?

ה * If ▬▬▬▬ צרעת and is deep in the skin then the person becomes טמא.

ו What does the Kohen do with clothing that has צרעת on it?

ז A woman is טמא for seven days if she gives birth to a ▬▬▬▬.

ח Name one of the קרבנות that is brought by someone who had צרעת.

ט What is one of things that you do to a house that is afflicted with צרעת? (14:42)

י What is one of the colors of צרעת that makes a house טמא?

כ Only the ▬▬▬▬ can decide if the צרעת is טמא or טהור.

ל צרעת can come if someone spoke ▬▬▬▬. (Rashi, 13:46)

Explain the *halachot* of לשון הרע. What are some of the excuses people use to speak לשון הרע? What can we do in order to refrain from speaking לשון הרע?

מ     Where is a person who has צרעת sent? (13:46)

נ     צרעת is referred to as a ▭▭▭.

ס     What is one of the types of צרעת called?

ע     What is the other קרבן that is brought by someone who had צרעת?

פ     How does the Torah say that צרעת has spread?

צ     Part of the קרבן for a מצורע is two ▭▭▭.

ק     What is אסור for a woman to touch after she gives birth to a baby? (12:4)

ר     צרעת can cover a person's body from his ▭▭▭ until his ▭▭▭. (13:12)

ש     How long does a woman have to wait to become טהור after she gives birth to a baby girl? To a baby boy?

ת     How are the *halachot* that apply to a מצורע referred to in the parsha? (14:2)

If a person has צרעת and completes his purification, he remains טמא until the Kohen proclaims that he is טהור. Why should this proclamation make the difference in his טהרה? After all, the person waited the proper amount of time and went to the מקוה.

פרשת תזריע and פרשת מצורע clarify the issues of צרעת. The purpose of צרעת is to cause a spiritual awakening in the sufferer so that he or she will be motivated to serve Hashem more seriously. In the *haftorah* of פרשת תזריע (*II Melachim* 4:42–5:19), Elisha cures Naaman from צרעת, but he does not ask for reward because his only interest is serving Hashem. The *haftorah* of פרשת מצורע (*II Melachim* 7:3–20) tells of four people who suffered from צרעת, but who demonstrated עבודת ה׳ by helping Benei Yisrael overcome the threat of Aram. (*II Melachim* 4:42–5:19; [*II Melachim* 7:3–20])

A person who becomes טמא must isolate himself for seven days. This gives him time to reflect on why he became טמא and how he can improve his behavior to ensure that it will not happen again. If we take the time to learn from our mistakes, then we too can improve our עבודת ה׳.

# אחרי מות
# ACHAREI MOT

**Parsha Points:**

▸ Aharon HaKohen receives instructions about what to do in the Mikdash on Yom Kippur. This includes the days of preparation before Yom Kippur as well as the קרבנות offered on Yom Kippur itself.

▸ The Kohen Gadol is instructed how to remain טהור during the עבודה on Yom Kippur.

## Questions

א * Which word in the parsha appears twice in four different פסוקים?

ב On Yom Kippur, the Kohen Gadol is ▭ ▭ ▭ מכפר. (16:6)

> What are the עשרת ימי תשובה? How do we do תשובה in preparation for Yom Kippur?

ג How does the Kohen Gadol decide the fate of each קרבן on Yom Kippur?

ד * The קטורת offered on Yom Kippur had to be ▭. (Rashi, 16:12)

ה Which two types of people are forbidden to do מלאכה on Yom Kippur?

ו What does Hashem promise to anyone who keeps the חקים and משפטים? (18:5)

> Define the different types of mitzvot. How many mitzvot are there? How many positive mitzvot? How many prohibitions?

ז * Which important מידה do we learn from the first פסוק in the parsha? (Rashi, 16:1)

ח Yom Kippur falls out on ▭.

ט What does the Kohen Gadol have to do before he changes his clothing on Yom Kippur?

> What is a מקוה? What kind of water is required for a kosher מקוה, and how much?

י From the word _____, we learn that someone who slaughters an animal outside the Mishkan and does not offer it as a קרבן is compared to a murderer. (Rashi, 17:4)

כ Someone who drinks the blood of an animal is _____ חייב. (17:10)

ל The Kohen did the עבודה on Yom Kippur _____ for the sins of Benei Yisrael.

מ Which עבודה זרה is discussed in the parsha?

נ Anyone who eats a _____ becomes טמא.

ס What was the main ingredient of the קטורת?

ע The mitzva of כסוי הדם requires us to cover the blood of an animal with _____ after it is slaughtered.

פ Another word for sin mentioned in the parsha is _____.

צ כסוי הדם is done to _____. (17:13)

ק Which room in the Mishkan was the Kohen Gadol allowed to enter on Yom Kippur?

ר Before the שעיר לעזאזל is sent into the מדבר, the Kohen does סמיכה on its _____.

ש Someone who is _____ animals without offering them as a קרבן in the Mishkan is compared to someone who is _____. (Rashi, 17:4)

ת Which words in the parsha teach us about the עינוים on Yom Kippur? (16:29)

List some of the עינוים of Yom Kippur.

**Parsha Puzzler**

Yom Kippur is the holiest day of the year, but it is the only day that the Kohen Gadol did not wear his בגדי זהב. Why not?

**Haftorah Highlights**

פרשת אחרי מות contains many mitzvot that teach moral and decent behavior. At the end of the parsha, Hashem informs Benei Yisrael that improper behavior can result in גלות. In the *haftorah*, the *navi* Amos describes Benei Yisrael's corrupt leadership and how they will be punished and sent into גלות. When Benei Yisrael do תשובה, Hashem will forgive them and bring them to Eretz Yisrael. (*Amos 9:7–15*)

**Learning Lesson**

Rashi says in 16:16 that Hashem promises that even when a person is טמא, the שכינה is still with him. Hashem is forgiving and patient. This teaches us to be tolerant and patient toward people who are different from us.

# קדושים
# KEDOSHIM

## Parsha Points:

▶ Benei Yisrael are expected to be קדושים, holy people who are different from other nations because of their special connection with Hashem.

▶ There are special *halachot* given to Benei Yisrael in order to help poor people, such as שכחה, לקט, and פאה.

▶ Many mitzvot are listed in the parsha, some of which are בין אדם לחברו such as ואהבת לרעך כמוך, and some that are בין אדם למקום such as שעטנז.

Questions

א    What is the second commandment in the parsha? And what is another word in the parsha for idols?

ב    How does the Torah instruct the בית דין to judge carefully?

ג    We must be careful not to torment a ▓▓▓▓▓ because ▓▓▓▓▓.

ד *    Which מידה do we learn from the words בצדק תשפט עמיתך? (Rashi, 19:15)

When and how have you applied this מידה?

ה    The mitzva to reprimand someone who is doing a sin is called ▓▓▓▓▓.

ו    Which words in the parsha are called a כלל גדול בתורה? (Rashi, 19:18)

Give personal examples of how this mitzva applies to you.

ז    How is Eretz Yisrael described the parsha?

ח    The Torah says not to curse a ▓▓▓▓▓ but the mitzva includes everyone. (Rashi, 19:14)

ט *    Give an example of someone we must save to keep the mitzva of לא תעמד. (Rashi, 19:16)

י    What is an עם הארץ supposed to do to someone who gives his children to the מולך?

כ    What is the איסור of crossbreeding animals or trees called?

ל    How do we know that one should not take revenge?

מ    The Torah says not to sacrifice one's child to an עבודה זרה called
       ▓▓▓▓▓. (Rashi, 19:34)

נ *   What do we learn about the generosity of Hashem from the
       words אני ה'? (Rashi, 19:17)

ס *   A person who gets used to stealing ▓▓▓▓▓. (Rashi, 19:11)

ע    How do you call fruits that are אסור to eat for the first three
       years?

פ    Which part of the field is one supposed to leave for poor
       people?

פ, צ * Clothing with שעטנז has ▓▓▓▓▓ and ▓▓▓▓▓ together.
       (Rashi, 19:19)

> Discuss the *halachot* of שעטנז. Are we allowed to try clothing
> on that has שעטנז in it? How do we avoid the problem of
> שעטנז today?

ק    Hashem commanded Benei Yisrael at the beginning of the
       parsha: ▓▓▓▓▓ ▓▓▓▓▓, which means פרושים תהיו – separate
       yourselves from certain things. (Rashi, 19:2)

ר    What is a person who gossips about others called?

> What is the difference between רכילות and לשון הרע?

ש    Name a person whom we are obligated to stand for.

> From what age is a person considered a שיבה? How long
> do we have to remain standing for an older person? Give
> examples of when we might have an opportunity to do this
> mitzva.

ת *   List four מצוות לא תעשה from the parsha and explain them.

**Parsha Puzzler**

Hashem commands Benei Yisrael: "קדושים תהיו," be holy. Define קדושה and how we can fulfill this mitzva.

**Haftorah Highlights**

In the *haftorah*, Yechezkel reprimands Benei Yisrael for not keeping many of the mitzvot that are in the parsha, such as being cruel to orphans and widows, desecrating Shabbat, speaking רכילות, and distorting justice. Fulfilling these mitzvot represents the way to fulfill קדושים תהיו. (*Yechezkel* 22:1–16 [*Yechezkel* 20:1–20])

**Learning Lesson**

The Torah says that קדושים תהיו was said to all of עדת בני ישראל. Within Benei Yisrael there are various types of people who see things differently. It is important to see past our differences and recognize that our common goal is to pursue קדושה.

**Parsha Points:**

▶ The Kohanim are given instructions on what they are and are not allowed to do in order to remain טהור.

▶ Benei Yisrael are instructed on how to count the *Omer,* how to offer the קרבן עומר for the new wheat, and how to offer the שתי הלחם, one of the special קרבנות offered on the festival of Shavuot.

Questions

א   A Kohen Gadol is not allowed to marry an ▓▓▓▓▓▓.

ב   If a ▓▓▓▓▓▓ ▓▓▓▓▓▓ marries a Yisrael she can no longer eat תרומה.

ג   Which woman is אסור for a Kohen to marry?

ד   How do we know that if you did not bring a קרבן on a festival, you cannot bring it the next day? (Rashi, 23:37)

> How does this *halacha* pertaining to קרבנות apply to תפילה? What is תשלומין, and how is it done?

ה*   Which word in the parsha demonstrates that there were ענני הכבוד, and why? (Rashi, 23:43)

ו   How do we know that we should use the ארבעת המינים on the festival of Sukkot?

ז   Rosh HaShana is referred to in the parsha as ▓▓▓▓▓▓.

ח   A person who was born from a Kohen who married a גרושה is called a ▓▓▓▓▓▓.

ט   A Kohen must be particularly careful not to become ▓▓▓▓▓▓.

י   What special day do we observe on the tenth day of the seventh month?

כ   One of the ways to sanctify a festival is by wearing a ▓▓▓▓▓▓. (Rashi, 23:35)

> Discuss the *halachot* of changing clothes לכבוד שבת. What does a person do if they do not have another garment to change into? Is one obligated to change shoes for Shabbat?

ל Why do we sit in the sukka for seven days? (23:43)

What else is the sukka supposed to remind us of, and why?

מ * What situation requires a Kohen to become טמא? (Rashi, 21:11)

נ What are the two ways that a person can obligate themselves to give a קרבן? (22:18)

When do we say התרת נדרים, and why?

ס Which mitzva do we still do today in order to remember the קרבן עומר?

When do we say ספירת העומר? What is the ברכה on ספירת העומר? What is the proper way to count the *Omer*, and what happens if you forget to count one day?

ע We sit in *sukkot* in order to remember the ▬▬▬. (Rashi, 23:43)

פ An etrog is called ▬▬▬. (23:40)

What makes an etrog kosher? What makes an etrog פסול?

צ A person can take a קרבן שלמים from his ▬▬▬. (22:21)

ק * What is another word for תרומה? (Rashi, 22:14)

ר The Kohen Gadol is instructed ▬▬▬ because he was anointed with oil on his ▬▬▬. (21:10)

ש What is another word for relatives of the Kohen?

ת The seventh month of the Jewish calendar is ▬▬▬.

**Parsha Puzzler**

What are the differences between a Kohen Gadol and a Kohen Hedyot?

**Haftorah Highlights**

פרשת אמר contains all of the laws that apply to the Kohanim. In the *haftorah*, these guidelines are repeated by the *navi* Yechezkel. (*Yechezkel* 44:15–31)

**Learning Lesson**

The Torah prohibits us from slaughtering a mother animal and her offspring on the same day. Many *Rishonim* explain that this teaches us sensitivity. If the Torah warns us to consider the feelings of an animal, then certainly we must be sensitive to people's feelings.

**Parsha Points:**

▸ שמיטה comes every seventh year. During this year, one is not allowed to work the land of Eretz Yisrael. This demonstrates that we believe that all our פרנסה comes from Hashem. יובל is the fiftieth year after seven שמיטה cycles. There are special *halachot* that apply to the יובל year, such as freeing all servants. In addition, any land that was purchased is returned to its original owner.

▸ Benei Yisrael are expected to be careful about how they conduct business. The laws of נשך and רבית prohibit a Jew from taking interest on loans.

## Questions

א   During the שמיטה year you are not allowed to work the ▓▓▓▓▓▓.

> Discuss some of the *halachot* of שמיטה that apply today in Eretz Yisrael.

ב   Which words teach us that the *halachot* of every mitzva were clarified at Har Sinai? (Rashi, 25:1)

ג   Someone who offers financial assistance to a poor relative is called a ▓▓▓▓▓▓.

ד   On the יובל year a ▓▓▓▓▓▓ is proclaimed throughout Eretz Yisrael freeing all servants. (25:10)

ה *   It is אסור to offer someone advice that is not ▓▓▓▓▓▓. (Rashi, 25:17)

ו   What is the ברכה that Benei Yisrael receive when they fulfill the mitzva of שמיטה? (25:18)

ז   What is one of the מלאכות that is אסור during שמיטה?

ח   How does the Torah refer to the support that is offered to the poor?

ט   If Benei Yisrael keep the שמיטה, than all will be ▓▓▓▓▓▓ in Eretz Yisrael.

י   What is the year after the seventh cycle of שמיטה called?

כ   During the שמיטה year, one is not allowed to prune his ▓▓▓▓▓▓. (25:4)

ל List two reasons why Benei Yisrael were taken out of Mitzrayim.

מ It is אסור for Benei Yisrael to offer קרבנות on a ▓▓▓▓▓▓ or an אבן ▓▓▓▓▓. (26:1)

נ What is another word in the parsha for preserved grapes? (Rashi, 25:11)

ס Fruits that were picked in the שמיטה year that grew the year before are called ▓▓▓▓▓. (25:11)

ע What type of work is אסור for a master to enforce on his servant? (25:39)

פ ▓▓▓▓▓▓ is when a master makes his servant do extra work for no reason. (Rashi, 25:43)

צ * ▓▓▓▓▓▓ means that Eretz Yisrael will not be sold or given away if Benei Yisrael keep the שמיטה properly. (Rashi, 25:23)

ק What is the Hebrew word for relative? (25:25)

ר If ▓▓▓▓▓ falls on a Shabbat, then we do not blow the shofar. (Rashi, 25:9)

ש The יובל year begins by blowing the ▓▓▓▓▓.

ת How many years pass between each יובל?

The Torah says that if שמיטה is not properly observed then Benei Yisrael will be sent out of Eretz Yisrael. Why is the punishment so severe? Why is the mitzva of שמיטה so important?

Chanamel, the nephew of the *navi* Yirmeyahu, was about to sell his land and lose his inheritance in Eretz Yisrael. The *haftorah* begins as Yirmeyahu pays the debt in order to redeem Chanamel's field. This is the mitzva of גאולת השדה described in the parsha. (*Yirmeyahu* 32:6–27)

If a poor person has to sell his field, the Torah says והשיגה ידו, he should not despair because he will find a solution. The Torah also confirms that the land will return to this person's family at the יובל. The Chafetz Chaim explains that although we may face difficulties in our lives, we should maintain a positive perspective.

**Parsha Points:**

▶ Hashem describes the reward Benei Yisrael will receive when they follow the Torah, and the horrible consequences they will suffer if they do not.

▶ Every year, when a person looks over the new animals born to his stock, he must put aside every tenth animal. The owner takes these animals to Yerushalayim, where he sacrifices them in the Beit HaMikdash and eats part of their meat in a state of purity. This mitzva is called מעשר בהמה.

Questions

א    What type of tree is the עץ השדה? (Rashi, 26:4)

ב    Hashem promised to make a ▒▒▒▒▒ with Benei Yisrael if they keep the mitzvot.

ג    What will fall in the right time if Benei Yisrael keep the mitzvot?

ד    If Benei Yisrael do not keep the mitzvot, then Hashem will send ▒▒▒▒▒. (26:25)

ה    Which animal must be offered on the מזבח as קדוש?

ו    What is the *halacha* if a person swears to donate to the Mishkan the amount of money equal to the value of his life, but he cannot afford to do so? (27:8)

ז    The monetary value of a ▒▒▒▒▒ varies according to age.

ח    Eretz Yisrael will become a ▒▒▒▒▒ if Benei Yisrael do not follow Hashem. (26:31)

ט    Once a person designates an animal as a קרבן, he cannot change that animal ▒▒▒▒▒. (27:10)

י*    Which words demonstrate that even old fruits will always taste fresh? (Rashi, 26:10)

כ*    When someone violates the ברית with Hashem, he is called a ▒▒▒▒▒ and a ▒▒▒▒▒. (Rashi, 26:15)

ל    Part of the ברכה for Benei Yisrael is that they will be full even after eating a small portion of ▒▒▒▒▒. (26:5)

מ    What is the mitzva called when one takes a portion of his fruit and eats it in Yerushalayim because it is קדוש?

נ    A person can make a ▨▨▨▨ to donate money to the Mikdash.

ס *    What type of punishment will Benei Yisrael receive if Hashem becomes disgusted with their behavior? (Rashi, 26:30)

ע    אם בחקתי תלכו means that we should be ▨▨▨▨. (Rashi, 26:3)

פ    If Benei Yisrael keep the mitzvot, then the trees will give ▨▨▨▨.

צ    What is a פקודה from Hashem? (Rashi, 26:16)

ק    How do you call the punishments that Hashem will give Benei Yisrael if they do not follow the Torah?

ר    One of the ברכות Hashem gave Benei Yisrael is that their enemies will ▨▨▨▨.

ש    What will Hashem give Benei Yisrael in Eretz Yisrael if they follow the mitzvot?

ת    The ▨▨▨▨ describes the punishments that Benei Yisrael will receive if they do not follow the mitzvot.

**Parsha Puzzler**

List all of the ברכות that Benei Yisrael will receive if they follow the mitzvot.

**Haftorah Highlights**

The parsha describes the ברכות Benei Yisrael will receive if they follow the Torah, as well as the קללות if they do not. The *navi* Yirmeyahu also relates to Benei Yisrael the קללות they will receive if they forsake Hashem. Yirmeyahu explains that only someone who trusts in Hashem will benefit from His ברכות. (*Yirmeyahu* 16:19–17:14)

**Learning Lesson**

According to the *Torat Kohanim,* אם בחקתי תלכו teaches us to be עמלים בתורה – to study Torah intensively. In order to achieve this, we must invest time and effort. This is especially true with spiritual values such as לימוד תורה and שמירת המצוות.

ספר במדבר

# SEFER BAMIDBAR

# במדבר

# BAMIDBAR

## Parsha Points:

▶ Hashem instructs Moshe to count the number of people in each שבט, except for שבט לוי.

▶ The Torah describes how Benei Yisrael camped around the Mishkan, which directions they found themselves in, and the flags and symbols that each שבט had.

▶ The Torah describes how Benei Yisrael traveled and transported the Mishkan during their travels in the מדבר. שבט לוי was in charge of carrying the Mishkan and its utensils and parts.

**Questions**

א * On which day did Hashem instruct Moshe to count Benei Yisrael? (Rashi, 1:1)

ב From where did Hashem speak to Moshe? (1:1)

ג Benei Yisrael were counted according to their ▭▭▭▭▭ , which means headcount. (1:2)

ד How did the שבטים know where to camp around the אהל מועד? (2:2)

ה When Benei Yisrael were traveling, Aharon and his sons covered the ▭▭▭▭▭ ארון with a פרוכת. (4:5)

ו What were the Levi'im warned not to do to the ארון and the מזבח while they were traveling? (4:15)

ז Only the ▭▭▭▭▭ were counted in Benei Yisrael.

ח From what age was Moshe instructed to count the בכור of each family?

ט * What do we learn from the fact that Zevulun and Yissachar became great תלמידי חכמים because they camped next to Moshe? (Rashi, 3:38)

י Moshe counted the men in each שבט who were ▭▭▭▭▭ .

כ The ארון was covered with a ▭▭▭▭▭ בגד. (4:6)

ל * All שבטים were counted ▭▭▭▭▭ and ▭▭▭▭▭ .

List the שבטים in their proper order.

מ Name three כלים that were covered with a בגד תכלת. (4:9–11)

What color is תכלת, and why do we have תכלת in tzitzit?

נ What were the leaders of each שבט called?

ס Where did the Levi'im camp? (1:50, 53)

ע Only men who were ▓▓▓▓▓ and older were counted.

פ What is another word for "counting" in the parsha?

צ Anyone who was twenty and older could be part of the ▓▓▓▓▓.

ק ▓▓▓▓▓ was responsible for carrying those כלים known as ▓▓▓▓▓. (4:4)

ר How are the נשיאים referred to in the Torah? (1:4)

ש What was used to count people? (Rashi, 1:2)

ת The tribes of Reuven, Shimon, and Gad camped in this direction.

**Parsha Puzzler**

Hashem instructs Moshe to count Benei Yisrael. Why was it so important for Benei Yisrael to be counted, and why at this particular time?

**Haftorah Highlights**

The *navi* Hoshea sinned when he suggested to Hashem to abandon Benei Yisrael. After he realized his mistake, Hoshea did תשובה by offering a ברכה to Klal Yisrael. The *haftorah* begins with his ברכה, which compares the multitudes of Benei Yisrael to the sand by the sea. פרשת במדבר begins with the counting of Benei Yisrael to demonstrate their numbers. (*Hoshea* 2:1–22)

**Learning Lesson**

When the Torah lists Aharon's children, it refers to them as "the children of Aharon and Moshe." Rashi comments that Moshe was considered a parent to Aharon's children because he taught them Torah. The Torah serves as the ideal way for the Jewish people to identify and unite as one family.

## Parsha Points:

▶ Moshe is instructed to count the families of the Levi'im.

▶ The נשיאים dedicate special קרבנות upon the completion of the Mishkan.

▶ A נזיר is someone who refrains from certain things, such as drinking wine, in order to get close to Hashem.

▶ Moshe gives Aharon the ברכת כהנים. These are the ברכות that the Kohanim, who are the messengers of Hashem, use to bless Benei Yisrael.

## Questions

א Which son of Aharon oversaw the work of משפחת גרשון? (4:28)

ב ________ is the special ברכה the Kohanim give to Benei Yisrael.

> Discuss the *halachot* of ברכת כהנים. When is it recited in Eretz Yisrael, and when is it recited in חוץ לארץ? What is the congregation supposed to do during ברכת כהנים, and why?

ג While a person is a נזיר, he has to ________ his hair, and when he completes his נזירות he has to ________ his hair.

ד* Hashem ________ to Moshe from on the כפורת, and Aharon was not included in the ________. (Rashi, 7:89).

ה What does the Kohen do to the סוטה with the water? (5:24)

ו What are Benei Yisrael instructed to do to a צרוע and a זב? (5:4)

ז It is prohibited for a נזיר to eat even the ________ of the grapes. (6:4)

ח* All of the נשיאים offered קרבנות in honor of the ________ ________.

ט* Name one of the people who the Torah says must remain outside the Machane Yisrael.

י What is אסור for a נזיר to drink?

כ How much קטורת was offered in each one of the קרבנות of the נשיאים?

ל* Singing and playing instruments was part of the עבודה of the ________ in the Mishkan. (Rashi, 4:47)

מ What did the סוטה drink? (5:18)

נ A man or a woman can become a _____ by making a _____ to Hashem.

ס Name part of the קרבן that a נזיר offers when he completes his term. (6:15)

ע Every two נשיאים had an _____, with one ox for every נשיא. (7:3)

פ * What did the Kohen do to the head of the סוטה, and why? (Rashi, 5:18)

צ What word in the parsha means covered?

ק * The _____ of the נשיאים was the only time the _____ was offered by individuals and on the מזבח החיצון. (Rashi, 7:14)

ר * This שבט was counted first, even though they did not travel first.

ש From what age were the Levi'im counted?

ת A כלי that a נזיר is not allowed to use.

**Parsha Puzzler**

The ברכת כהנים starts with יברכך. What is the difference between receiving a ברכה and receiving protection from Hashem?

**Haftorah Highlights**

The parsha contains all the laws regarding a נזיר. In the *haftorah*, a מלאך ה′ instructs a woman to follow the laws of a נזיר because she and her husband, Manoach, would have a son who would become a נזיר. Manoach and his wife follow the instructions of the מלאך, and they are blessed with a son called Shimshon. (*Shoftim* 13:2–25)

**Learning Lesson**

Although all of the קרבנות that the נשיאים offered were the same, the Torah lists the name and קרבן of each נשיא. This teaches us that everything we do for Hashem is important even if it is not unique.

# בהעלותך
# BEHAALOTCHA

**Parsha Points:**

▶ Aharon is instructed by Hashem how to light the מנורה.

▶ Moshe is instructed by Hashem to make trumpets out of silver. These trumpets were used to inform Benei Yisrael that they would travel, to gather the leaders of the שבטים, and to gather Benei Yisrael to offer sacrifices on festivals and in times of need.

▶ Hashem gave Benei Yisrael the מן to eat while they were in the מדבר. Benei Yisrael complained about the מן and claimed that they wanted meat. Hashem sent them a type of bird called a שלו, and anyone who ate from it was killed as a punishment from Hashem.

▶ Miriam and Aharon spoke לשון הרע about Moshe. Miriam was punished and received צרעת for speaking לשון הרע. Benei Yisrael were commanded by Hashem to remember what happened to Miriam and to avoid speaking לשון הרע.

Questions

א    How did Aharon position himself to light the מנורה?

ב    Which ארון journeyed three days ahead of Benei Yisrael?

ג    A ▬▬▬▬ is obligated to keep Pesach just like all of Benei Yisrael.

ד    Yissachar and Zevulun traveled as part of ▬▬▬▬.

ה *    How did Moshe know how to build the מנורה? (Rashi, 8:4)

ו    Which words in the parsha do we say when we take the Torah out of the ארון?

> What is the proper way to take leave from the ארון קודש after returning the ספר תורה?

ז    One of the ways Benei Yisrael expressed their desire to return to Mitzrayim. (11:5)

ח *    Moshe was told by Hashem to make two ▬▬▬▬.

ט    What did the מן fall onto?

> Which mitzva do we perform on Shabbat to remember the מן? What is the proper way to fulfill this mitzva?

י    Hashem was ▬▬▬▬ to Moshe ten times. (Rashi, 11:17)

כ    What were the חצוצרות made out of?

ל    What was the first thing Benei Yisrael did with the מן every weekday morning?

מב What were the people who complained about the מן called?

Discuss the concept of הכרת הטוב.

ג Moshe was told to gather seventy זקנים to receive _____ as one.

ס In order to sanctify the Levi'im, Benei Yisrael did _____ to the Levi'im, and the Levi'im did _____ to their קרבנות עולה and קרבנות חטאת.

ע How does the Torah describe Moshe?

פ How did Hashem talk to Moshe? (12:8)

צ _____ was called an אישה כושית, which means that she was beautiful. (Rashi, 12:1)

ק The people who complained about the מן died in _____.

ר What does the word עם refer to in the parsha? (Rashi, 11:1)

ש Which birds did Benei Yisrael eat after they complained about the מן?

ת How did Benei Yisrael know when they should begin to travel in the מדבר?

**Parsha Puzzler**

Moshe was instructed to make two silver trumpets. When and for what occasions were these trumpets used?

**Haftorah Highlights**

The parsha opens with a description of how Aharon should light the מנורה. In the *haftorah*, the *navi* Zecharya describes a vision of a מנורה. The light of this מנורה represents the leadership of Zerubavel, which is strengthened by emulating the spirituality of Hashem. (*Zecharya* 2:14–4:7)

**Learning Lesson**

The word בהעלתך comes from the root of לעלות, which is to rise upward. Rashi comments that the flame ignited from the מנורה would straighten out and point heavenward. This portrays the importance of striving to grow upward, and that the path to righteousness is through Torah.

# שלח
# SHLACH

▶ Benei Yisrael decide to send the leader of each שבט as מרגלים. The מרגלים would spy on Eretz Canaan to see if it was a good land.

▶ When the מרגלים return from Eretz Canaan, all of them report bad things about the land to Benei Yisrael, except for Yehoshua and Kalev, who say good things. The מרגלים, and those people who listened to them, were punished, and they died before they could enter Eretz Canaan.

▶ A person desecrates Shabbat in the מדבר, and he is killed through stoning.

▶ Benei Yisrael are given the mitzvot of challa and tzitzit. Challa is a person's obligation to give a portion of dough to the Kohen each time he makes bread. Tzitzit is what we wear on a four-cornered garment.

Questions

א  The word ▨▨▨▨▨ refers to important people. (Rashi, 13:3)

ב  How did the מרגלים begin their report about Eretz Canaan? (13:27)

ג  Hashem told Moshe that He would destroy Benei Yisrael and make Moshe into a ▨▨▨▨▨.

ד  The מרגלים spoke ▨▨▨▨▨, which means they gave a bad report about Eretz Yisrael.

> Let's prove the מרגלים wrong. Discuss the positive and beautiful things that Eretz Yisrael has to offer.

ה  Which mitzva is described in Bamidbar 15:20?

> Discuss the *halachot* of הפרשת חלה as they apply today.

ו  "▨▨▨▨▨ כלב" means that he remained silent.

ז  What was the positive description the מרגלים gave about Eretz Canaan?

ח *  Which איסור was the מקושש עצים doing?

> Describe some of the מלאכות of Shabbat. Offer some practical examples of what would be considered חילול שבת today.

ט  Two מרגלים told Benei Yisrael regarding Eretz Canaan: מאד מאד ▨▨▨▨▨ ▨▨▨▨▨. (14:7)

י, כ  Who were the two מרגלים who did not speak badly about Eretz Canaan?

ל    Which word in the parsha means to spy?

מ *  The ▓▓▓▓ was ▓▓▓▓ Shabbat, and his punishment was
     ▓▓▓▓ ▓▓▓▓.

נ    What did Benei Yisrael say when they heard a negative report
     about Eretz Canaan from the מרגלים? (14:4)

ס    Moshe prayed to Hashem ▓▓▓▓ for Benei Yisrael, and
     Hashem responded ▓▓▓▓. (14:19–20)

ע    Who were the נפילים? (Rashi, 13:33)

פ, צ *  There is a ▓▓▓▓ ▓▓▓▓ on every corner of the ▓▓▓▓.

> When is one obligated to wear tzitzit? What size do they
> have to be? What material should they be made of? Who is
> obligated to wear them? What ברכה do we make on tzitzit?

ק    What did Yehoshua and Kalev do after Benei Yisrael said that
     they wanted to return to Mitzrayim? (14:6)

ר    How did Hashem instruct Moshe to kill a מחלל שבת? (15:35)

ש    A person who sins by mistake is called a ▓▓▓▓.

ת *  What is the numerical value of the word tzitzit plus eight strings
     and five knots? (Rashi, 15:39)

At the beginning of the parsha, Hashem tells Moshe to send the מרגלים to spy on Eretz Canaan. If the מרגלים were instructed to spy on Eretz Canaan, what was their sin?

After the negative report of the מרגלים, Benei Yisrael were discouraged from conquering Eretz Canaan. In the *haftorah*, Yehoshua sends two מרגלים to Eretz Canaan in order to help enable Benei Yisrael to conquer the land and to fulfill the mitzva of Hashem. The report that these מרגלים gave to Yehoshua upon their return was that Hashem had handed the land over to Benei Yisrael. (*Yehoshua* 2:1–24)

The majority of the נשיאים were מרגלים who spoke badly about Eretz Canaan. Yehoshua and Kalev encouraged Benei Yisrael to believe in Hashem and enter Eretz Canaan regardless of the widespread disapproval. Sometimes we are influenced to behave the wrong way by our peers. Yehoshua and Kalev demonstrated strength because they did not follow the majority. They followed their own understanding of what Hashem expected from them.

**Parsha Points:**

▶ Korach rebels against Hashem by challenging Moshe for the leadership of Benei Yisrael. Korach and his followers are killed by Hashem.

▶ Hashem gives two signs to Moshe to demonstrate that only Moshe is the leader of Benei Yisrael.

▶ Hashem informs Aharon of the twenty-four special gifts that a Kohen receives.

▶ The parsha talks about the mitzva of פדיון הבן. When someone's first child is a boy, after thirty days, he gives the Kohen money and redeems the value of the child.

## Questions

א    He is one of the three people whose name is mentioned as part of עדת קרח.

ב    Korach felt that the  ▓▓▓▓▓  ▓▓▓▓▓ received too much כבוד.

ג    Where is wheat gathered after it is cut? (18:27)

ד    This is another person who is mentioned as part of עדת קרח in the parsha.

ה    How did Moshe refer to Korach and his followers? (17:26)

ו*   From these words we learn that Korach separated himself and persuaded the leaders of the שבטים to rebel against Moshe. (Rashi, 17:1)

ז*   An ▓▓▓▓▓ איש, who is not from ▓▓▓▓▓, is not permitted to offer the קטורת.

ח*   What happened to Aharon's staff? (Rashi, 17:23)

ט*   Korach challenged Moshe by asking him if a ▓▓▓▓▓ needs tzitzit. (Rashi, 16:1)

> Discuss the *halachot* of a טלית גדול. When is it worn? Who wears it? What is the ברכה we make on a טלית גדול?

י    Who prayed that his name should not be mentioned with Korach's name? (Rashi, 16:1)

כ    Korach and his עדה told Moshe that ▓▓▓▓▓. (16:3)

ל A ⬛⬛⬛ is also obligated to give part of his portion to a Kohen.

מ How did Hashem punish Benei Yisrael after they followed Korach?

נ The מעשר that the Levi'im receive is their ⬛⬛⬛. (18:26)

ס What did Moshe instruct Benei Yisrael to do with regard to Korach? (16:26)

ע The group who followed Korach were called an ⬛⬛⬛.

פ Which mitzva does a person perform for his oldest child when the child is one month old?

Who has to have a פדיון הבן? How do we do a פדיון הבן, and on which day after the baby is born?

צ What grew out of Aharon's staff in the אהל מועד? (17:23)

ק Who was Korach's grandfather?

ר What is one of the complaints that Korach had against Moshe and שבט לוי?

ש In order for a person to redeem their firstborn, they had to give five ⬛⬛⬛. (18:16)

ת What is the portion of fruit that Benei Yisrael have to give to the Kohen every year?

## Parsha Puzzler

What are the different types of תרומה that Benei Yisrael are required to offer? To whom are they offered, and when?

## Haftorah Highlights

Korach's rebellion was not for the sake of serving Hashem but rather for his own personal interests. In the *haftorah*, the *navi* Shmuel informs Benei Yisrael that because of their requests to have a king, he would appoint Shaul. However, Shmuel reminded Klal Yisrael that they must continue serving Hashem and the Torah. (*I Shmuel* 11:14–12:22)

## Learning Lesson

Korach was interested in personal recognition. This haughtiness led to his downfall. One of the most important מידות that we must have is ענוה, humility. A person who is humble will always remember that Hashem is above him, and he will be careful to behave properly.

# חוקת
# CHUKAT

**Parsha Points:**

▶ Hashem instructs Benei Yisrael of the פרה אדומה, the red cow. The פרה אדומה is burned, and its ashes are used to purify someone who has come into contact with a dead person, who is known as a טמא מת.

▶ Moshe is told by Hashem to build a copper snake. Anyone who is bitten by a real snake can look up at the copper snake, remind themselves of their belief in Hashem, and, in this way their lives will be saved.

▶ Both Edom and Sichon confront Benei Yisrael with war. With Hashem's help, Benei Yisrael are victorious and consequently pass through to the bank of the Jordan River.

## Questions

א   The first mitzva in the parsha is ▓▓▓▓ פרה.

ב   The Kohen who burns the פרה אדומה must wash his ▓▓▓▓ and ▓▓▓▓.

ג   Edom would not allow Benei Yisrael to pass through its ▓▓▓▓. (20:21)

ד   Which words demonstrate that Benei Yisrael promised Edom that they would not wander off of the main road? (Rashi, 20:17)

ה   Where did Aharon die?

ו   How does the Torah describe Moshe's sin? (20:11)

ז   Where do we learn that Benei Yisrael will perform all the mitzvot even if they do not understand the reason for some of them? (Rashi, 19:2)

ח   Which type of כלי becomes טמא inside if it is exposed to a dead person? (Rashi, 19:15)

ט   After the first time Moshe hit the rock, only ▓▓▓▓ of water came out. (Rashi, 20:11)

י   How did Hashem inform Moshe that Aharon would die and not enter Eretz Yisrael? (20:24)

כ   Who cried and mourned after Aharon died? (20:29)

ל   What was Edom's response after Benei Yisrael asked to travel through their land? (20:18)

ב What became the name of the place where Moshe sinned after Benei Yisrael complained that they had no water?

ג After Benei Yisrael complained that they had no food or water, Hashem sent a ▨▨▨▨, and many people were killed. Hashem told Moshe to make a ▨▨▨▨ to save Benei Yisrael.

ס Which king would not allow Benei Yisrael into his land and waged war against them?

ע When Aharon died, the ▨▨▨▨ stopped surrounding Benei Yisrael. (Rashi, 21:1)

פ What is the first mitzva in the parsha?

צ, ק Miriam died in ▨▨▨▨ מדבר, in the city of ▨▨▨▨. (20:1)

ר After Moshe hit the rock, how much water came out?

ש If the פרה אדומה has ▨▨▨▨, it cannot be used as a פרה אדומה. (Rashi, 19:2)

ת The Torah says about anyone who touches someone טמא: ▨▨▨▨. (19:22)

Why is it that when the Kohen purifies someone through the ashes of the פרה אדומה the Kohen himself becomes טמא?

Haftorah Highlights

In פרשת חוקת, Sichon attacks Benei Yisrael en route to Eretz Yisrael. Moshe leads Benei Yisrael to battle, and they successfully conquer Sichon's land, which originally belonged to Moav. In the *haftorah*, the king of Amon attempts to capture these lands that belonged to Moav. Once again, he is defeated by Benei Yisrael under the leadership of Yiftach HaGil'adi, whom the *navi* describes as a mighty warrior. (*Shoftim* 11:1–33)

Learning Lesson

Rashi comments (20:29) that when Aharon died, all of Benei Yisrael cried because he preserved and encouraged שלום בית. Aharon understood that respect and love for one another would help keep families close together. It is important for us to appreciate our families as well as our extended family of Benei Yisrael.

# בלק
# BALAK

**Parsha Points:**

▸ Balak, the king of Moav, sends Bilam to curse Benei Yisrael.

▸ On the way to curse Benei Yisrael, Bilam's donkey is miraculously given the gift of speech. It tries to discourage Bilam from fulfilling his mission. Bilam does not listen and continues on his destructive mission.

▸ Hashem causes Bilam to bless Benei Yisrael instead of cursing them.

Questions

א    What was Balak's incentive for cursing Benei Yisrael? (22:6)

ב    Whom did Balak send to curse Benei Yisrael?

ג    Which word teaches us that Bilam wanted to wipe out Benei Yisrael from this world? (Rashi, 22:11)

ד*    Name the מלך ישראל who will destroy Moav. (Rashi, 24:17)

ה    How do we know that Benei Yisrael live apart from other nations? (23:9)

ו*    How do we know that Bilam hated Benei Yisrael and was eager to destroy them? (Rashi, 22:21)

ז    The ▬▬▬ and the ▬▬▬ came to Bilam to ask him to curse Benei Yisrael. (22:7)

ח    What did Bilam say to the angel?

ט    One of the ways that Benei Yisrael show their eagerness to serve Hashem is by wearing a ▬▬▬. (Rashi, 23:24)

י    Bilam blessed Benei Yisrael that they would have plenty of water, by saying ▬▬▬. (24:7)

כ    Bilam wanted Balak to give him all of his ▬▬▬. (Rashi, 22:18)

ל    What were the two instructions that Hashem gave to Bilam before he decided to curse Benei Yisrael? (22:12)

מ    What is one of the praises that Bilam said about Benei Yisrael that is part of our תפילה every morning?

## When do we recite this תפילה, and why?

ג  Moav was afraid of Benei Yisrael because they heard about all of the _____ that Hashem did for them.

ס  Moav and Midyan said that Benei Yisrael would wipe out everything _____. (22:4)

ע  How did the messengers who went to Bilam refer to Benei Yisrael?

פ  Which type of עבודה זרה did Balak want Benei Yisrael to worship?

צ  Balak was the son of _____.

ק  What did the זקני מדין and זקני מואב have in their hands for Bilam when they came to him for the first time?

ר  When the donkey saw the מלאך ה', he pressed Bilam's _____ against the wall.

ש  The donkey complained that Bilam hit him _____. (22:28)

ת  Hashem told Bilam that whatever He would decide, _____ אותו and _____ אותו. (22:20, 35)

**Parsha Puzzler**

When Bilam describes Benei Yisrael at the beginning of the parsha, he refers to them as "the nation *coming out* of Mitzrayim." Why does Bilam use the present tense, when Benei Yisrael had already left Mitzrayim?

**Haftorah Highlights**

The *navi* Micha warns Benei Yisrael against עבודה זרה. Micha refers to the parsha and reminds Klal Yisrael of Balak and Bilam's plot to entice Benei Yisrael to sin. The *haftorah* concludes as Micha reminds Benei Yisrael to follow the ways of Hashem through משפט, חסד, and צניעות. (*Micha* 5:6–6:8)

**Learning Lesson**

Bilam was discouraged by Hashem, the מלאך, and his own donkey from cursing Benei Yisrael, but he did not listen. Bilam was determined to fulfill his own mission, although it was destructive and corrupt. We should be determined to complete positive goals that involve יראת שמים and עבודת ה'.

# פנחס

# PINCHAS

**Parsha Points:**

- Zimri, the head of שבט שמעון, commits a tragic sin by living with Kozbi, a princess of Midyan.

- Aharon's grandson Pinchas kills Zimri for the act he committed and is rewarded by Hashem for doing so.

- Hashem instructs Moshe to divide Eretz Yisrael into twelve portions for the twelve שבטים. The daughters of Tzelofchad from שבט מנשה receive a portion of Eretz Yisrael as well.

Questions

א   Pinchas was the son of ▓▓▓▓▓▓, who was the son of ▓▓▓▓▓▓.

ב   What did Pinchas receive from Hashem? (25:12)

ג   How was Eretz Yisrael divided up among the שבטים?

ד   Who are the two רשעים from שבט ראובן mentioned in the parsha?

ה   ▓▓▓▓▓▓ חג is called ▓▓▓▓▓▓ יום. (Rashi, 28:26)

ו   What are Benei Yisrael instructed to do on Yom Kippur? (29:7)

Discuss the עינוים of Yom Kippur. What are some of the special mitzvot we do on Yom Kippur?

ז   The earth swallowed up Korach and his followers to teach us that a ▓▓▓▓▓▓ should not argue with a Kohen. (Rashi, 26:10)

ח   What is the festival of Sukkot called in the Torah?

ט*  Moshe was told to warn Yehoshua that Benei Yisrael were ▓▓▓▓▓▓ and stubborn, to ensure that Yehoshua would understand them. (Rashi, 27:19)

י   Who was appointed to succeed Moshe?

כ   Name one of the איסורים that applies to all of the festivals. (28:18)

ל   What is one of the complaints the daughters of Tzelofchad expressed to Moshe? (27:4)

מ*  According to one opinion, Tzelofchad was the ▓▓▓▓▓▓ who was ▓▓▓▓▓▓. (Rashi, 27:3)

נ    What did the daughters of Tzelofchad want?

ס    What did Hashem instruct Moshe to do to Yehoshua?

ע    How does the Torah refer to the festival of Simchat Torah?

פ    One of the reasons why Benei Yisrael were instructed to destroy the Midyanim was because they encouraged Benei Yisrael to worship the ▧▧▧▧▧.

צ    Moshe wanted to appoint a successor because he did not want Benei Yisrael to be like ▧▧▧▧. (27:17)

ק    Which words teach us that Pinchas avenged שם ה'? (Rashi, 25:11)

ר    Moshe counted the ▧▧▧▧ of every male over twenty to know the number of people in each שבט.

ש    How did Hashem instruct Moshe and Elazar to count Benei Yisrael? (26:2)

ת    One of the daughters of Tzelofchad was called ▧▧▧▧.

When the Torah introduces Pinchas, it says: "Pinchas, son of Elazar, son of Aharon the Kohen." Why does the Torah have to specify Pinchas's lineage?

Pinchas killed Zimri, a נשיא who desecrated the name of Hashem. This discouraged Benei Yisrael from straying from the דרך ה'. In the *haftorah*, the *navi* Eliyahu challenges the רשעים King Achav and Queen Izevel, who tried to spread עבודה זרה throughout Eretz Yisrael and tried to kill the נביאי ה'. According to one opinion in Chazal, Pinchas was the *navi* Eliyahu. Eliyahu also challenged Achav and Izevel to encourage Benei Yisrael to follow the ways of Hashem. (*I Melachim* 18:46–19:21)

The daughters of Tzelofchad came to Moshe and requested a portion of Eretz Yisrael. Moshe did not know the *halacha* and had to ask Hashem for the answer. Rashi notes that in *Devarim* 1:17 Moshe instructs Benei Yisrael to bring any difficult questions to him. Moshe's intentions were to help Benei Yisrael, but he sounded too confident. Therefore, Rashi explains, Moshe forgot the *halacha*, because Hashem wanted to teach him a lesson in modesty. Even Moshe Rabbeinu, who was the most modest person, had to be reminded by Hashem not to be overly confident. From this we can learn the importance of being modest.

# מטות

# MATOT

▶ Moshe informs Benei Yisrael of the laws regarding נדרים. נדרים are oaths that a person takes in Hashem's name, and because they are in Hashem's name he is required to fulfill them.

▶ Moshe informs Benei Yisrael of the laws regarding the kashrut of utensils.

▶ The שבטים of Gad and Reuven request to settle in the Yarden, or Jordan Valley, rather than cross over to Eretz Yisrael. Hashem grants their request on the condition that they are the first to fight for Benei Yisrael in order to conquer Eretz Yisrael.

Questions

א    Who instructed Benei Yisrael how to purify themselves and their possessions when they return from war?

ב    What was one of the items that Benei Yisrael had to purify after they returned from war?

ג    Name one of the שבטים that wanted to settle outside Eretz Yisrael.

ד    What was the first city that בני גד built for themselves called? (32:34)

ה    What did Benei Yisrael do to the kings of Midyan and to Bilam ben Be'or? (31:8)

ו*    Which word in the parsha demonstrates how much Benei Yisrael loved Moshe and did not want to see him die? (Rashi, 31:5)

ז    Moshe was angry at Benei Yisrael because in the war with Midyan they killed only the ▬▬▬▬.

ח    How many מלכים did Midyan have?

ט    Whom did בני גד and בני ראובן want to build cities for? (32:16)

י    A father can annul the oath of his daughter on ▬▬▬▬ ▬▬▬▬. (30:6)

כ    What did the people offer to Hashem from the valuables they took from Midyan? (31:50)

ל  בני גד and בני ראובן would have to be ▮▮▮▮ when the nation conquers Eretz Canaan. (32:17)

מ  Half of ▮▮▮▮ שבט also settled with בני גד and בני ראובן.

נ  What are the first *halachot* that appear in the parsha?

Discuss the *halachot* of התרת נדרים. When and how do we do התרת נדרים? What special תפילה do we say during the year to nullify נדרים that the congregation may have taken, and when?

ס, ע  Moshe gave Reuven, Gad, and half of Menashe the lands of ▮▮▮▮, king of the Emori and ▮▮▮▮, king of the Bashan.

פ  Who led Benei Yisrael out to war against the Midyanim? (31:6)

צ  What kind of men did Moshe instruct Benei Yisrael to send out to war with the Midyanim? (Rashi, 31:3)

ק*  ▮▮▮▮ was one of the cities rebuilt and renamed by בני ראובן.

ר  Moshe related the *halachot* of נדרים to the ▮▮▮▮ first to show them respect. (Rashi, 30:2)

ש  A person can make a נדר or a ▮▮▮▮.

ת  Moshe told בני גד and בני ראובן to first help conquer Eretz Canaan and then ▮▮▮▮. (32:22)

**Parsha Puzzler**

In 31:8, the Torah lists the names of the kings of Midyan who were killed by Benei Yisrael and then says that they were five kings. Why does the Torah have to tell us that they were five kings? The Torah lists their names! Shouldn't that be enough for us to know how many kings there were?

**Haftorah Highlights**

This *haftorah* does not relate to the parsha, but rather to the time of year that it is read. פרשת מטות is read between Shiva Asar BeTammuz and Tisha B'Av, which is the time of year that we mourn the destruction of the Beit HaMikdash. The *haftorah* is taken from the book of *Yirmeyahu* and describes the חורבן הבית and the גלות that Benei Yisrael experienced afterward. (*Yirmeyahu* 1:1–2:3)

**Learning Lesson**

When the שבטים of Reuven and Gad asked Moshe to allow them to settle עבר הירדן, they said, "We shall build pens for our animals and cities for our small children." Reuven and Gad spoke first about their animals and then about their children. The Midrash criticizes them for worrying about their animals first and then showing concern for their children. We have to be careful to concentrate on the important things before we worry about things that are not as important. This will help us lead productive lives.

### Parsha Points:

▸ Hashem divides Eretz Yisrael and instructs Moshe as to where the borders of the country are.

▸ Moshe designates עָרֵי מִקְלָט throughout Eretz Yisrael. These cities are used for the sake of someone who murders another by mistake and needs to seek refuge in order to save himself from those relatives of the murdered person who may seek revenge.

Questions

א    ▨▨▨▨ died ▨▨▨▨ after Benei Yisrael came out of Mitzrayim. (33:38)

ב    What are two descriptions the Torah gives for how someone can kill someone else unintentionally? (35:22)

ג*    Someone who kills someone else by mistake is ▨▨▨▨. This way the ▨▨▨▨ cannot harm him, unless he leaves the ▨▨▨▨ of the city. (Rashi, 35:23)

ד    Part of the lands of Mitzrayim, Edom, and Moav were all next to each other in the ▨▨▨▨ of Eretz Yisrael. (Rashi, 34:3)

ה    Where did Aharon die?

ו    What are two mitzvot that Benei Yisrael have to do with regard to living in Eretz Yisrael? (33:53)

> Discuss the mitzva of ישוב ארץ ישראל as it applies today.

ז    What did Moshe say to Benei Yisrael when he finished describing the boundaries of Eretz Yisrael? (34:13)

ח    The Torah describes the travels of Benei Yisrael in the מדבר to show that they had time to rest. This demonstrates the ▨▨▨▨ of Hashem. (Rashi, 33:1)

ט    When Benei Yisrael came out of Mitzrayim, the Mitzrim were ▨▨▨▨ because they were still burying their dead from the מכת בכורות. (Rashi, 33:4)

י    Eretz Yisrael is a ▨▨▨▨ for Benei Yisrael.

ב  A person in an עיר מקלט can go free when the ▓▓▓▓ ▓▓▓▓ dies.

ל  Who were given forty-eight cities to live in? (35:7)

מ  When did Benei Yisrael's first journey, which is recounted in the parsha, take place?

נ  What is the southern edge of the western border of Eretz Yisrael?

ס  Name two deserts mentioned in the parsha.

ע *  Someone who kills someone else by mistake can run to the ▓▓▓▓ ▓▓▓▓ and be safe.

פ  From Eitam, where did Benei Yisrael travel?

צ  How did Hashem begin instructing Moshe to tell Benei Yisrael about conquering Eretz Yisrael? (34:2)

ק  Where were the people who complained about food buried? (33:16)

ר  Someone who kills even by mistake is called a ▓▓▓▓ .

ש *  There were עָרֵי מִקְלָט ▓▓▓▓ situated מֵעֵבֶר לַיַּרְדֵּן and ▓▓▓▓ in Eretz Yisrael, which makes a total of ▓▓▓▓ .

ת  If there is killing in Eretz Yisrael, then people transgress two אִסּוּרִים: אֶת הָאָרֶץ ▓▓▓▓ לֹא and אֶת הָאָרֶץ ▓▓▓▓ לֹא. (35:33, 34)

## Parsha Puzzler

Why does the Torah need to repeat a list of all of the places Benei Yisrael traveled through in the מדבר? The Torah already says the names of the places as Benei Yisrael came to each place.

## Haftorah Highlights

This *haftorah* does not relate to the parsha, but rather to the time of year that it is read. פרשת מסעי is read between Shiva Asar BeTammuz and Tisha B'Av, which is the time of year that we mourn the destruction of the Beit HaMikdash. The *haftorah* is taken from the book of *Yirmeyahu* and describes the חורבן הבית and the גלות that Benei Yisrael experienced afterward. (*Yirmeyahu* 2:4–28, 3:4 [4:1–2])

## Learning Lesson

פרשת מסעי sums up all of Benei Yisrael's travels. The last פסוק of the parsha and of ספר במדבר is: "These are the commandments and laws that Hashem commanded through Moshe to Benei Yisrael." Perhaps the Torah wants us to understand that no matter where we go or what we do, the important thing is that we take with us the laws and commandments of Hashem, because that is what will ensure our strength and continuity.

ספר דברים

# SEFER DEVARIM

# דברים

# DEVARIM

## Parsha Points:

▶ Moshe reprimands Benei Yisrael for the times in the מדבר that they rebelled against Hashem.

▶ Benei Yisrael are instructed not to add on or take away from the mitzvot.

## Questions

א   Which words demonstrate that Moshe was about to reprimand Benei Yisrael? (Rashi, 1:1)

ב   On which day did Moshe address Benei Yisrael? (1:3)

ג   Which word in the parsha means border? (3:16, 17)

ד   When Benei Yisrael left Edom, they traveled ▨▨▨▨. (2:8)

ה   What did Moshe tell the people when he realized they were too many for him to handle?

ו   List four actions that the מרגלים did when they went to spy on Eretz Canaan. (1:24)

ז   Which word at the beginning of the parsha is a place where Benei Yisrael stopped in the מדבר and also reminds them of the sin they committed with the עגל הזהב? (Rashi, 1:1)

ח   Moshe was told to ▨▨▨▨ Yehoshua because he would become the next leader. (1:38)

ט   What was Benei Yisrael's reaction after Moshe told them to gather wise men to assist in leadership? (1:14)

י   Har Se'ir was a ▨▨▨▨ that would belong to Esav. (2:5)

כ   Moshe compared the numbers of Benei Yisrael to the ▨▨▨▨.

ל   What did the messengers promise Sichon that Benei Yisrael would not do? (2:27)

מ   Benei Yisrael took part of the land from the two ▨▨▨▨

whose land was on the other side of the Yarden. Their land stretched ▬▬▬. (3:8)

נ     ▬▬▬ is also referred to as the ▬▬▬. (1:7)

ס, ע     Moshe spoke to Benei Yisrael after he defeated ▬▬▬ and ▬▬▬, who lived in ▬▬▬. (1:4)

פ *     What was Og called, and why? (Rashi, 3:11)

צ     What kind of people did Moshe assemble to help him lead Benei Yisrael? (Rashi, 1:13)

ק     It takes eleven days to walk from Chorev to ▬▬▬.

ר     What was the part of the land that Hashem promised Avraham called? (Rashi, 3:13)

ש     How long did it take for Benei Yisrael to walk from Kadesh Barnea to Nachal Zered?

ת     Moshe told Benei Yisrael that anything that is difficult for them to judge ▬▬▬. (1:17)

Our parsha begins, אלה הדברים אשר דבר משה. What kind of words are דברים, and what do they refer to in the parsha?

פרשת
דברים

and this *haftorah* are always read on the Shabbat before Tisha B'Av, the day on which we commemorate the destruction of the Beit HaMikdash. The *navi* Yeshayahu describes the appearance of Eretz Yisrael after the destruction of Yerushalayim and the Mikdash. He reprimands Benei Yisrael for offering sacrifices insincerely and inciting the anger of Hashem. Yeshayahu encourages Benei Yisrael to do תשובה and envisions Eretz Yisrael's redemption. (*Yeshayahu* 1:1–27)

Moshe has harsh words to tell Benei Yisrael as he reminds them of their disobedient behavior. Rashi on 1:3 comments that Moshe delayed delivering these harsh words and reprimanded Benei Yisrael as he approached the end of his life instead, so as not to embarrass them. Moshe Rabbeinu teaches us that even when someone deserves to be criticized, we need to be sensitive to them.

# ואתחנן
# VAETCHANAN

## Parsha Points:

▶ Moshe prays to Hashem to allow him to enter Eretz Yisrael.

▶ Moshe reviews the עשרת הדברות – the Ten Commandments – with Benei Yisrael.

▶ The Torah introduces the mitzva of mezuza.

Questions

א   What did Moshe request from Hashem at the beginning of the parsha? (3:25)

ב   Moshe asked to see the Levanon, which is the ▭. (Rashi, 3:25)

ג   Benei Yisrael are referred to as a ▭. (4:7, 8)

ד*   What type of language does the Torah use when it instructs us to converse about the Torah בשכבך ובקומך? (Rashi, 6:7)

ה*   Yerushalayim is referred to as ▭. (Rashi, 3:25)

ו   Which פסוק in the parsha do we say after we finish reading from the Torah?

> Explain what הגבהה is. Discuss when הגבהה is done and the proper way to do it.

ז   Eretz Yisrael is also called ▭ ארץ. (6:3)

ח   Which famous mountain in Eretz Yisrael is mentioned in the parsha? (4:48)

ט   What is the tefillin worn on the head called? (Rashi, 5:8)

> Who is obligated to wear tefillin? What ברכה do we make on tefillin?

י   Where else are tefillin worn?

כ   How does the Torah instruct us to respect our parents?

ל* The Torah tells us to keep the mitzvot not just according to what they say but also ▓▓▓▓▓. This means that we have to try to do even more than what is written in the Torah. (Rashi, 6:18)

> Discuss and offer some possibilities on how we can behave לפנים משורת הדין.

מ We place ▓▓▓▓▓ on our doorposts.

> What does a mezuza have inside of it? On which side of the doorpost do we hang the mezuza? What do some people do when they walk by a mezuza?

נ How does the Torah promise Benei Yisrael that they will defeat their enemies? (7:1)

ס We are not allowed to make a פסל or any ▓▓▓▓▓. (4:16)

ע In this parsha, the Torah repeats the ▓▓▓▓▓.

פ How did Hashem speak to Benei Yisrael from Har Sinai? (5:4)

צ One of the directions Moshe was told to look toward.

ק How does the Torah instruct us to tie tefillin on our arm?

ר Where does Moshe go to see Eretz Yisrael in all directions? (3:27)

ש What does Benei Yisrael have to do in order to survive and inherit Eretz Yisrael? (4:1)

ת One cannot add on to a mitzva because it says ▓▓▓▓▓ לא, nor can one take away from a mitzva because it says ▓▓▓▓▓ לא. (4:2)

> Offer examples of how a person could transgress these two איסורים.

The opening word of the parsha is ואתחנן. What does the word ואתחנן mean, and why did Moshe use it at this particular time? The פסוק says "at that time"; which time is Moshe referring to?

This haftorah is the first of the seven haftarot of comfort that are taken from the navi Yeshayahu. These haftarot are read to comfort Benei Yisrael after Tisha B'Av, when we commemorate the destruction of the Beit HaMikdash. Yeshayahu talks about the reconstruction of Yerushalayim and how Hashem will embrace Benei Yisrael in Eretz Yisrael. The haftorah opens with the words: "נחמו עמי," and the Shabbat of פרשת ואתחנן, therefore, has become known as שבת נחמו. (Yeshayahu 40:1–26)

פרשת ואתחנן contains the first parsha of קריאת שמע, which says ושננתם לבניך – You shall teach (Torah) thoroughly to your children. Rashi comments that the word "children" often refers to students. This demonstrates a lesson to both parents and teachers. Parents have to view their children as students and teach them proper lessons for life. Teachers have to care for their students as if they were their own children.

## Parsha Points:

▶ Benei Yisrael are given the mitzva of saying ברכת המזון after they eat.

▶ The Torah praises the attributes and beauty of Eretz Yisrael.

▶ The Torah introduces the mitzva of tefillin.

א  How does the Torah describe Eretz Yisrael in the parsha? (8:9)

ב  When Benei Yisrael follow the mitzvot, then the Jewish nation will be ▩▩▩▩. (7:14)

ג  Benei Yisrael must love a ▩▩▩▩ because ▩▩▩▩. (10:19)

ד  What will Benei Yisrael collect if they worship Hashem? (11:14)

ה*  From the mitzva of יראת ה', we learn ▩▩▩▩. (Rashi, 10:12)

ו  Which words in the parsha teach us the mitzva of ברכת המזון?

> Discuss the *halachot* of ברכת המזון. Where do you have to say ברכת המזון? How much bread do you have to eat in order to say ברכת המזון? How long can one wait to say ברכת המזון after he has finished eating?

ז  One of the תפילות that Moshe prayed to Hashem was ▩▩▩▩. (9:27)

ח  Hashem provides Benei Yisrael with the strength to do ▩▩▩▩. (8:18)

ט  What kind of land is Eretz Yisrael?

> Discuss the attributes of Eretz Yisrael and what makes the country special. Why is Eretz Yisrael special to you?

י  The rain that falls on seeds after they were planted is called ▩▩▩▩. (Rashi, 11:14)

כ  When Benei Yisrael are victorious in war, what should they refrain from saying? (8:17)

ל   Moshe said that when he was on Har Sinai receiving the Torah, ▓▓▓▓. (9:18)

מ   Which words in the parsha teach us that the mitzvot should be new to us every day? (Rashi, 11:13)

נ   We are supposed to worship Hashem with all of our heart and all of our ▓▓▓▓. (11:13)

ס   Which word in the parsha means to leave the ways of the Torah? (Rashi, 11:16)

ע *   What is תפילה called? (Rashi, 11:13)

What are the different תפילות called, and what are their time frames?

פ   How did Hashem instruct Moshe to prepare the second set of לוחות? (10:1)

צ *   Which insect could throw poison and cause blindness? (Rashi, 7:20)

ק   The second paragraph of ▓▓▓▓ is in the parsha.

When and how many times a day is one obligated to say the קריאת שמע? Explain the כוונה that is needed when reciting the קריאת שמע and the way one should carefully articulate the words and letters of the קריאת שמע.

ר, ש   Two of the seven species of Eretz Yisrael are ▓▓▓▓ and ▓▓▓▓.

What are the שבעת המינים and what ברכה אחרונה do you say on them? If you have all of the שבעת המינים, in what order should you make the ברכה ראשונה, and what should you eat first?

ת   What mitzva should a person do even בלכתך בדרך?

**Parsha Puzzler**

The Torah directs us "to love Hashem, to walk in His ways, and to cling to Him." What does the Torah mean? How are we supposed to "cling" to Hashem?

**Haftorah Highlights**

This *haftorah* is the second of the seven *haftarot* of comfort that are taken from the *navi* Yeshayahu. Yeshayahu refers to Hashem as a mother who never forgets her children. He reminds the Jewish people that if they renew their allegiance to the way of Avraham and Sara, Hashem will comfort Tziyon and restore Eretz Yisrael to its glory. (*Yeshayahu* 49:14–51:3)

**Learning Lesson**

The Torah paints the following scenario in the parsha: "Your heart will become haughty and you will forget Hashem…. And you may say in your heart, my strength and the strength of my hand made me all this wealth. Then you should remember Hashem, Who gave you the strength to make wealth."

On the one hand, we have to believe that all of our abilities come from Hashem. However, we cannot sit back and wait for Him to help us. We have to work and invest effort in order to become successful. This combination of believing in Hashem, but at the same time contributing actively to society, is maintained only when we keep our "hearts from becoming haughty."

# ראה

# RE'EH

▶ Moshe instructs Benei Yisrael to destroy idols or anything used for עבודה זרה and to be careful not to erase the name of Hashem.

▶ Benei Yisrael are given the signs for kosher animals and fish, as well as a list of kosher birds.

▶ Benei Yisrael are instructed not to cook meat and milk together. This is the basis for the prohibition of eating meat and milk together.

▶ There are different types of מעשר that Benei Yisrael have to give. Some מעשר goes to the Kohanim, some to the Levi'im, and some to the poor people.

▶ Benei Yisrael are instructed to give צדקה to poor people.

Questions

א    Which words teach us that Benei Yisrael have to destroy all עבודה זרה when they enter Eretz Yisrael? (12:2)

ב, ג    The ▨▨▨ that Hashem gave to Benei Yisrael was given on the mountain called ▨▨▨. (11:29)

ד    Which part of an animal is אסור to eat?

ה    How does the Torah say not to sacrifice animals outside of the Mikdash? (12:13)

ו    List the four promises that Hashem tells Benei Yisrael regarding conquering and settling Eretz Yisrael. (12:10)

ז    Who is obligated to go to the Beit HaMikdash on Pesach, Shavuot, and Sukkot? (16:16)

ח    What is another name for a false prophet? (13:6)

ט    A non-kosher animal is referred to as ▨▨▨, and a kosher animal is referred to as ▨▨▨.

י    What is the נחלה that Benei Yisrael will receive? (Rashi, 12:9)

כ *    Anyone who believes in עבודה זרה is ▨▨▨. (Rashi, 11:28)

ל    Which פסוק teaches us that you cannot cook or eat meat and milk together?

> Which things do we have around the kitchen to separate meat and milk? How long do we have to wait between eating meat and milk? What do we have to do after eating milk, in order to eat meat?

מ *     Give the two signs of a kosher animal.

נ     A false prophet is called a ▮▮▮▮▮.

ס     What are the two signs of a kosher fish?

ע     From which mountain did Hashem give Benei Yisrael a קְלָלָה? (11:29)

פ, צ     What does the Torah instruct us to do in order to help poor people? What is this mitzva called? (15:11)

> What are the different ways to give צדקה, and what is the most preferred way?

ק     When the Torah says that Benei Yisrael have to be an ▮▮▮▮ עַם, it means ▮▮▮▮. (Rashi, 14:21)

ר     On the ▮▮▮▮ שלש, we are not allowed to come to the Mikdash ▮▮▮▮. (16:16)

ש     What is the word מנוחה referring to in the parsha? (Rashi, 12:9)

ת     The phrases ▮▮▮▮ לֹא and ▮▮▮▮ לֹא teach us that it is אסור to mourn too much for someone who died. (14:1)

The Torah warns us not to listen to a false prophet or a dreamer even if he or she produces an אות or a מופת. What is the difference between a prophet and a dreamer and between an אות and a מופת?

This haftorah is the third of the seven haftarot of comfort that are taken from the navi Yeshayahu. Yeshayahu refers directly to the restoration of מלכות בית דוד. The nations of the world will recognize the greatness of Hashem and His divine covenant with Benei Yisrael. (Yeshayahu 54:11–55:5)

פרשת ראה contains the mitzva of צדקה: "If there shall be a poor person among you in any of your cities…you shall not harden your heart or close your hand." Rashi comments, based on the Midrash, that from the words "among you" we learn that the poor people in your city should be cared for before the poor of other cities. Sometimes we focus on others and forget those close to us in our community or even our family. Before we try to save the world we have to help the people closest to us.

# שופטים
# SHOFTIM

## Parsha Points:

▶ Hashem tells Benei Yisrael to appoint judges and officers to help ensure justice.

▶ The judges appointed by Benei Yisrael are instructed to judge honestly and to treat all Jewish people fairly.

▶ The mitzva of ראשית הגז requires a Jew to give the first shearings of his lamb to a Kohen.

▶ Benei Yisrael are given instructions with regard to a מלחמת מצוה. This is a war that is a mitzva to engage in, such as conquering Eretz Yisrael.

▶ It is prohibited for Benei Yisrael to cut down fruit-bearing trees in Eretz Yisrael.

## Questions

א A tree that is worshiped for עבודה זרה is called an _____. (16:21)

ב For what kind of court cases would a person go to a בית דין? (17:8) What is one of the reasons why someone is exempt from going to war? (20:5)

ג, ד Two gifts that a person has to give a Kohen are the first of the _____ from his animal and the first of his _____. (18:4)

ה* *Devarim* 19:14 describes what we call _____.

ו What is a בית דין supposed to do to someone who worships עבודה זרה? (17:5)

ז What is one of the things that a מלך ישראל cannot have a lot of?

ח A false witness is called an _____ עד. (19:16)

ט* When Benei Yisrael fight another nation, they are not allowed to kill the _____. (Rashi, 20:14)

י We have to follow the decision of a בית דין even if they say _____. (17:11)

כ Why can't Benei Yisrael destroy trees when they are fighting another nation? (20:19)

ל Benei Yisrael can destroy a tree only if they know that _____. (20:20)

מ This is a מזבח made of one stone upon which Benei Yisrael are not allowed to offer sacrifices. (Rashi, 16:22)

ג Give another reason why someone is exempt from going to war. (20:6)

ס A מלך ישראל is not allowed to have too many ▬▬▬▬▬.

ע Witnesses who testify falsely against other witnesses are called ▬▬▬▬▬.

פ What is the reason Benei Yisrael have to prepare roads to get to an עיר מקלט? (Rashi, 19:6)

צ How do we know that a person should try to find a reliable Jewish court of law? (Rashi, 16:20)

ק It is אסור for a Jew to be a witch or a ▬▬▬▬▬. (18:10)

ר Someone who kills another person is called a ▬▬▬▬▬. (19:3)

ש Which two kinds of people are Benei Yisrael instructed to have in the communities they live in?

ת How do we know that we are supposed to accept what Hashem gives us without investigating the future? (18:13)

**Parsha Puzzler**

The Torah instructs Benei Yisrael to listen to all that the חכמים tell them. Rashi quotes Sifri as saying: "Even if the חכמים seem to tell you that your right is left and your left is right." How can this be? Are we expected to listen to the חכמים even when it seems clear that what they are saying is wrong?!

**Haftorah Highlights**

This *haftorah* is the fourth of the seven *haftarot* of comfort that are taken from the *navi* Yeshayahu. Here, the *navi* describes how upset Hashem is that Benei Yisrael are in גלות. However, Hashem reassures Benei Yisrael that He will lead them and protect them. (*Yeshayahu* 51:12–52:12)

**Learning Lesson**

Benei Yisrael are instructed to appoint שופטים and שוטרים in all of their cities. This appears to be a communal obligation. However, the commentary *Sefat Emet* understands this instruction to be a personal obligation incumbent upon every Jew. The שופטים, or judges, refer to our obligation to constantly "judge" or work on our relationship with Hashem, and the שוטרים, or officers, refer to our responsibility to dedicate ourselves to Torah. This is why it says in the פסוק: "*You* shall appoint judges and officers in your cities" instead of "*They* shall appoint."

**Parsha Points:**

▶ Benei Yisrael are warned about different types of relationships that are unhealthy. These relationships can lead to trouble in the Jewish family, like having a בן סורר ומורה, a rebellious son.

▶ The Torah informs Benei Yisrael about the mitzva of השבת אבידה, returning lost items.

▶ The parsha delineates many more mitzvot, such as שעטנז – the prohibition against mixed breeding; שילוח הקן – the obligation to send away a mother bird before taking her eggs; and מעקה – building a fence around one's roof to ensure that people will not fall and hurt themselves.

▶ Amalek attacked Benei Yisrael as soon as they came out of Mitzrayim. Benei Yisrael must remember what Amalek did, and it is a mitzva to destroy the nation of Amalek.

א    What is the first topic addressed in the parsha?

ב    What is the rebellious son in the parsha called?

ג, ד *    A woman is not allowed to wear clothing of a ▓▓▓▓ in order to be ▓▓▓▓ to a man. (Rashi, 22:5)

ה, ו    How does the Torah warn about צרעת? (24:8)

ז *    Which two mitzvot in the parsha have to do with remembering?

ח    It is אסור for a ▓▓▓▓ to do ▓▓▓▓ together with an ox. (22:10)

ט    Name one thing we are not allowed to ask for with regard to Amon or Moav. (23:7)

י    Which mitzva does a younger brother perform when he marries the widow of his older brother?

כ    The איסור of planting two species together in a field or a vineyard is called ▓▓▓▓.

ל    Which איסור is repeated for the sake of protecting poor people? (Rashi, 24:17)

מ    What does a person have to build around their new house?

נ    The איסור of taking interest is called ▓▓▓▓. (23:20)

ס *    A rebellious son is called a ▓▓▓▓ בן because he is ▓▓▓▓. (Rashi, 21:18)

ע Which nations are never allowed to convert and become part of Klal Yisrael?

פ, צ Which two materials are אסור to mix when making a garment?

ק How do we know that one should bury the dead as quickly as possible? (21:23)

Explain the concept of כבוד המת. Explain what חברה קדישא and טהרה are.

ר A firstborn receives a double portion because he is ▓▓▓▓▓▓. (21:17)

ש Which mitzva in the parsha instructs us to remove a mother bird before taking her eggs?

ת How does the Torah tell us to destroy Amalek? (25:19)

How many types of כלאים are listed in the parsha, and what are they?

Haftorah Highlights

This haftorah is the fifth of the seven haftarot of comfort that are taken from the book of Yeshayahu. It is also the same haftorah as פרשת נח. The navi Yeshayahu tells Benei Yisrael that tragedies such as the מבול, the חורבן הבית, and the גלות have a purpose. Their purpose is to encourage תשובה and to strengthen Benei Yisrael's commitment to Hashem. (Yeshayahu 54:1–10)

Learning Lesson

The Torah says that we are not allowed to reject or persecute a person from Mitzrayim because the Mitzrim hosted us there when we were slaves. Even though the Mitzrim were cruel to us and enslaved us, the Torah still demands that we be sensitive to the fact that they were our hosts, even if it was under terrible conditions. This demonstrates the importance of appreciating assistance even when it comes under strange circumstances. If we are expected to be sensitive to the Mitzrim who enslaved us, how much more so do we need to be sensitive to one another.

# כי תבוא
# KI TAVO

## Parsha Points:

▸ Benei Yisrael are given the mitzva of ביכורים. The first fruits of the harvest are brought to Yerushalayim during the period between Shavuot and Sukkot, and they are given as a gift to a Kohen.

▸ Moshe and the זקנים are instructed to inscribe the mitzvot on slabs of rock and place them on Har Eival. These slabs will remind Benei Yisrael of their commitment to the Torah as they pass through the Yarden.

▸ Moshe informs Benei Yisrael of the curses they will receive if they do not follow the mitzvot.

## Questions

א Which parsha is recited when offering the ביכורים? (26:5)

ב, ג All of the ________ were given from ________ הר. (27:12)

ד Name one of the קללות that Benei Yisrael will receive if they do not follow the Torah. (28:22)

ה* What does a person say to show that the fruit in his field is ביכורים? (Rashi, 26:2)

ו What happened after Mitzrayim enslaved Benei Yisrael? (26:7)

ז, ח* One of the ברכות says that Benei Yisrael will be head of the nations and not the ________ and will leave this world without any ________. (Rashi, 28:6, 13)

ט What holds the ביכורים?

י Which ברכה means that Hashem will help Benei Yisrael become a holy nation? (28:9)

כ Benei Yisrael are obligated to give ביכורים after ________. (Rashi, 26:1)

ל* ________ wanted to ________ everything. (Rashi, 26:5)

מ* Someone who is ________ his father or mother means that he is ________ them, and consequently he is cursed. (Rashi, 27:16)

נ What will Hashem place in front of Benei Yisrael's enemies in order to protect them? (28:7)

ס    One of the kings mentioned at the end of the parsha who waged war against Benei Yisrael.

ע    Upon which mountain were the curses declared?

פ    What will Benei Yisrael feel in their hearts if they are cursed? (28:67)

צ    One of the ברכות given to Benei Yisrael is that their flocks of ▬▬▬ will be blessed. (28:4)

ק    Name another of the קללות that Hashem will send upon Benei Yisrael if they do not follow the Torah. (28:22)

ש, ר*  The ביכורים are the ▬▬▬, and are only offered from the ▬▬▬ ▬▬▬. (Rashi, 26:2)

ת *  Which mitzva is included in the פסוקים that describe the mitzva of מעשר? (Rashi, 26:13)

List three examples of ברכות that Moshe gave Benei Yisrael and what they mean.

This *haftorah* is the sixth of the seven *haftarot* of comfort that are taken from the book of *Yeshayahu*. The *navi* Yeshayahu informs Benei Yisrael that all of them will be righteous, which will in turn give them strength and hasten the arrival of the Mashiach. (*Yeshayahu* 60:1–22)

Moshe instructed Benei Yisrael to engrave the mitzvot on a stone and to set the stone on Har Eival, the mountain from which Benei Yisrael heard the curses. This teaches us that even when times are tough and the Jewish people are struggling, and even when it seems like Hashem has abandoned us, we are still obligated to follow the mitzvot and believe in Hashem. It may be easier to follow Hashem during productive and happy times, but the test of בטחון is to continue to believe in Hashem even during trying and difficult times.

## Parsha Points:

▶ Moshe addresses Benei Yisrael before he dies. He tells them to learn Torah and says that everyone is capable of learning Torah.

## Questions

א    Which mitzva is described in the last פסוק of the parsha?

ב *    Moshe calls Benei Yisrael together ▬▬▬▬ ▬▬▬▬ to make a ▬▬▬▬. (Rashi, 29:9)

ג    When Benei Yisrael pass through the lands of the ▬▬▬▬, they will see their ▬▬▬▬. (29:15, 16)

ד    Moshe makes a ברית with the people who were living as well as with the ▬▬▬▬. (Rashi, 29:14)

ה, ו    How does the Torah say that Hashem will bring Benei Yisrael to Eretz Yisrael, and what will happen after Benei Yisrael arrive there? (30:5)

ז    Name one group of people who stood in front of Hashem.

ח    Which is one of the types of גרים described at the beginning of the parsha? (29:10)

ט    The children who stood in front of Hashem for the ברית are called ▬▬▬▬.

י    Our forefathers were ▬▬▬▬ Eretz Yisrael, and we will too. (30:5)

כ    Which words in the parsha show that the תורה שבכתב and the תורה שבעל פה are accessible to Benei Yisrael? (Rashi, 30:14)

ל    Which words in the parsha demonstrate that the Torah is not far away from us? (30:12)

מ    Who gathered Benei Yisrael to make a ברית with Hashem? (Rashi, 29:9)

ג   Name another group of people who stood in front of Hashem.

ס, ע   If Benei Yisrael do not follow the Torah then their land will be destroyed just like ▓▓▓▓ and ▓▓▓▓. (29:22)

פ   How does the Torah warn Benei Yisrael not to stray from Hashem and worship עבודה זרה? (29:17)

צ *   Hashem promises to be with Benei Yisrael even when they experience ▓▓▓▓ ▓▓▓▓. (Rashi, 30:3)

ק   Where in the parsha does it show that Hashem will gather Benei Yisrael from גלות? (30:3)

ר, ש   Name another two groups of people who stood in front of Hashem.

ת   Which mitzva is described in 30:1–5?

**Parsha Puzzler**

In *Devarim* 30:11, the Torah says: "For *this* commandment that I command you today – it is not hidden from you and it is not distant." Which commandment is the Torah referring to?

**Haftorah Highlights**

This *haftorah* concludes the seven *haftarot* of comfort following Tisha B'Av. The *navi* Yeshayahu relates how Hashem will take revenge on Edom and the rest of Benei Yisrael's enemies. The *haftorah* closes as Yeshayahu speaks of the pain that Hashem also experiences when Benei Yisrael are in גלות, and how Hashem will redeem them. (*Yeshayahu* 61:10–63:9)

**Learning Lesson**

The parsha begins as Moshe says: "You are standing today before Hashem; the heads of your tribes, your elders, your officers, all of the men of Yisrael." Moshe could have addressed all of the men of Yisrael without specifying different types of people. Rashi comments that Moshe listed the most important people first, and after that the rest of Benei Yisrael. This teaches us that the Torah and the ברית we make with Hashem are just as binding for the simple man as for a leader or a person of great stature. The Torah offers the opportunity for anyone to develop a relationship and connect with Hashem, regardless of the position they hold.

## Parsha Points:

▸ Moshe informs Benei Yisrael that Yehoshua will be the next leader and that Yehoshua will take them into Eretz Yisrael.

▸ Benei Yisrael receive the mitzva of הקהל. At the end of the שמיטה year, everyone gathers in the Beit HaMikdash to listen to the reading of the Torah.

▸ There is a special mitzva for a מלך ישראל to write a ספר תורה.

א    Where did Hashem tell Moshe and Yehoshua to stand? (31:14)

ב    Moshe gave over his last words ▭. (31:30)

ג    Even the ▭ was obligated to hear the words of the Torah so that he would fear Hashem.

ד, ה \* The reading for the mitzva of ▭ starts with פרשת ▭. (Rashi, 31:11)

ו    The parsha starts by telling us ▭ משה ▭.

ז    Hashem promises that the Torah will never be forgotten by Benei Yisrael and ▭. (Rashi, 31:21)

ח    What does Moshe instruct Yehoshua to do?

ט    Who was brought by their parents to the mitzva of הקהל?

י    ▭ would be the one to bring Benei Yisrael over the ▭. (31:2, 3)

כ \* How does Hashem say that He will deliver Benei Yisrael to Eretz Yisrael? (31:20)

ל    What is the purpose of the mitzva of הקהל? (31:12)

מ    How old was Moshe when he spoke to Benei Yisrael?

נ    The ▭ came to הקהל in order to hear the words of the Torah. (Rashi, 31:12)

ס    During which festival was the mitzva of הקהל observed?

ע, פ   The ▨▨▨▨ was hovering ▨▨▨▨. (31:15)

צ   Hashem warned that if Benei Yisrael do not follow the Torah, He would ignore the ▨▨▨▨ that they might experience. (Rashi, 31:17)

ק   How did Hashem instruct Moshe to call Yehoshua in order for him to become the new leader? (31:14)

ר   If Benei Yisrael do ▨▨▨▨, then Hashem will be angry. (31:29)

ש   During Sukkot immediately after which year is the mitzva of הקהל observed?

ת   What was the מלך ישראל told to do for the mitzva of הקהל? (31:11)

Why was the mitzva of הקהל done immediately after the שמיטה year?

פָּרָשַׁת וַיֵּלֶךְ is usually read on שבת שובה, which is the Shabbat between Rosh HaShana and Yom Kippur. Therefore, the *haftorah* is taken from the book of *Hoshea*, as the *navi* encourages Benei Yisrael to do תשובה and return to Hashem. There are references in the *haftorah* to וידוי (confessing one's sin, which is a main element of תשובה), offering קרבנות, and blowing the shofar, all steps that lead toward doing תשובה. (*Hoshea* 14:2–10 [*Micha* 7:18–20; *Yoel* 2:11–27])

The opening פסוק of the parsha says that "Moshe went." It is unclear where he went. Rav Moshe Feinstein explains that this is not referring to an actual place that Moshe went to, but rather to the influence Moshe had on the Jewish people. Moshe was about to die, but even after he would no longer be physically present, his influence would continue to exist and affect the Jewish world. Therefore, when the Torah says that Moshe went, it means that his influence would go on, even after he died.

# האזינו
# HAAZINU

## Parsha Points:

▶ Moshe sings a song to Benei Yisrael about how the Jewish people began and about the future of Jewish history.

## Questions

א    How are the *nevi'im* referred to in the parsha? (Rashi, 32:7)

ב    Name one type of animal that Benei Yisrael will offer for קרבנות. (32:14)

ג    Who will sing praises about Benei Yisrael? (32:43)

ד    ▓▓▓▓▓ would come out of stones in Eretz Yisrael. (32:13)

ה    How does Hashem express with wonder that Benei Yisrael should never challenge Him? (32:6)

ו    How will Hashem react if Benei Yisrael ignore Him? (32:19)

ז, ח    ▓▓▓▓▓ refers to the ▓▓▓▓▓. (Rashi, 32:7)

ט    The Torah is compared to ▓▓▓▓▓. (32:2)

י    How does it say that Benei Yisrael accepted the Torah in the מדבר? (32:10)

כ    Hashem will have mercy on Benei Yisrael ▓▓▓▓▓. (32:11)

ל*    How does פסוק מז encourage intense Torah learning? (Rashi, 32:47)

מ    The Torah is compared to ▓▓▓▓▓. (32:2)

נ    Upon which mountain did Moshe die?

ס    In Eretz Yisrael, honey would come out of the ▓▓▓▓▓. (32:13)

ע    The teachings of Hashem will fall like rain drops on ▓▓▓▓▓ ▓▓▓▓▓ and ▓▓▓▓▓ ▓▓▓▓▓. (32:2)

פ    What is one word in the parsha that refers to Hashem's deeds and actions? (32:4)

צ    How is Hashem referred to in the parsha? (32:4)

ק *   Hashem used שמים and ארץ as witnesses because they are ▓▓▓▓▓▓ ▓▓▓▓▓▓. (Rashi, 32:1)

ר *   What is another word for raindrops? (Rashi, 32:2)

ש, ת   ▓▓▓▓▓▓ ▓▓▓▓▓▓ refer to the fruits of Eretz Yisrael. (Rashi, 32:13)

**Parsha Puzzler**

Why did Moshe use שמים and ארץ as witnesses to what he was going to say?

**Haftorah Highlights**

פרשת האזינו is a song that Moshe offers to Benei Yisrael regarding their relationship with Hashem. The *haftorah* is also a song, but it is a personal one. David HaMelech praises and thanks Hashem for all of the miracles he was privileged to witness in his lifetime. (*II Shmuel* 22:1–51)

**Learning Lesson**

At the end of the parsha, Hashem instructs Moshe to ascend the mountain as He informs Benei Yisrael that Moshe will die in the middle of the day. Rashi says that Benei Yisrael did not want Moshe to die, and wanted to stop him from ascending the mountain. Yet many times Benei Yisrael confronted Moshe and insisted that he return them to Mitzrayim. They also complained about Moshe and his leadership many times. Unfortunately, only as Moshe nears his death do we see how much Benei Yisrael valued him. It is unfortunate when we learn to appreciate people only after they are no longer with us. We have to appreciate the people around us when they are alive, and when we have the opportunity to benefit from their presence before it is too late.

**Parsha Points:**

▸ As Moshe nears his death, he offers a ברכה to every שבט in Benei Yisrael.

▸ Moshe goes to the top of Har Nevo and, before he dies, Hashem shows him all of Eretz Yisrael.

▸ The Torah confirms that there never was and never will be a *navi* as great as Moshe Rabbeinu.

Questions

---

א    How is Moshe referred to at the beginning of the parsha?

---

ב    Most of the parsha records the ▇▇▇▇ that Moshe gave to ▇▇▇▇ ▇▇▇▇.

---

ג    What are fruits that grow from the moonlight? (Rashi, 33:14)

---

ד*    Which word in the parsha refers to old age? (Rashi, 33:25)

---

ה    Hashem showed Moshe all of Eretz Yehuda until ▇▇▇▇. (34:2)

---

ו    How do we know that Moshe was the greatest *navi* ever? (34:10)

---

ז*    Which שבט had sea merchants? (Rashi, 33:18)

---

ח    How do we know that Hashem will protect שבט בנימין? (33:12)

---

ט    We know that Asher's portion in Eretz Yisrael had a lot of oil because it says ▇▇▇▇. (33:24)

---

י    Who became the leader of Benei Yisrael after Moshe?

---

כ    Which sea in Eretz Yisrael did Naftali receive as part of his portion? (Rashi, 33:23)

---

ל    What does the Torah say about the burial place of Moshe Rabbeinu? (34:6)

---

מ    Moshe died in the land of ▇▇▇▇, and he was buried ▇▇▇▇.

---

נ*    Moshe died when Hashem gave him a ▇▇▇▇. (Rashi, 34:5)

ס    How did Moshe appoint Yehoshua as the new leader? (34:9)

ע    What title did Moshe receive when he passed away?

פ    The Torah says that Moshe spoke with Hashem ▓▓▓▓▓.

צ    What kind of קרבנות will Benei Yisrael offer on the mountains of Yissachar and Zevulun? (33:19)

ק    No one knows where Moshe's ▓▓▓▓▓ is.

ר    What was Yehoshua filled with after he was appointed by Moshe?

ש    How many days did Benei Yisrael mourn for Moshe?

ת    Yericho is also called the city of ▓▓▓▓▓. (34:3)

### Parsha Puzzler

Hashem wrote the Torah and Moshe wrote it down. In 34:7 it says that Moshe died. However, there are still five פסוקים left until the end of the text of the Torah. If Moshe wrote the Torah, how could he have written the last few פסוקים when he was already gone?

### Haftorah Highlights

פרשת וזאת הברכה is always read on Shemini Atzeret and/or Simchat Torah. Therefore, the *haftorah* is not for the parsha, but rather for those of Shemini Atzeret and/or Simchat Torah. (*I Melachim* 8:54–66/*Yehoshua* 1:1–18)

### Learning Lesson

Moshe dies, but the Torah immediately declares that Yehoshua became the leader of Benei Yisrael. Even in a time of mourning, the Torah delivers a message that continuity is most important. Benei Yisrael mourn for the great Moshe Rabbeinu, and they are given a new leader to begin a new phase in history. This is how the Torah ends, because the same is true with Torah. There is no end to Torah, and although one might think that they know enough and have finished learning it, they must continue and learn more because they will surely find more insight and knowledge.

בראשית

Questions

א. אחד  ב. בשר  ג. גיהנום  ד. דעת ודיבור  ה. הבל  ו. ויהי טוב
ז. זרוע  ח. חנוך  ט. טרם יצמח  י. יהי אור  כ. כי טוב  ל. למך (רש״י
ד:כג)  מ. מים, מלח, מנחה (רש״י)  נ. נע ונד  ס. סיון  ע. עזר כנגדו
פ. פרי  צ. צלע  ק. קדם  ר. רועה צאן  ש. שת  ת. תמרים

---

ד — In the שמונה עשרה, we say the ברכה: "אתה חונן לאדם דעת ומלמד לאנוש בינה," in which we thank Hashem for giving us the power to think and express our thoughts. One has to be careful not to speak about others and to avoid דברים בטלים, which is talking about things for no purpose. To avoid these trappings, we should use our mouths productively through תפילה and תלמוד תורה. The more we are involved in productive things, the less time we have to waste.

מ — The קרבן מנחה is the least expensive of the קרבנות, and therefore it is generally offered by poor people. It consists of flour, oil, and different spices.

Parsha Puzzler

Even though Creation is hard to understand or to imagine, Hashem wanted Benei Yisrael to understand that He created the world. That is the first belief a Jew must have. According to the Ramban, we are taught the events that transpire in ספר בראשית with all of our forefathers to help us learn the concepts of דרך ארץ – proper behavior. These ideas are important to live by, and therefore precede the mitzvot.

א. אריה ב. ברכה ג. גופר ד. דגים ה. הוצא ו. וירד ה' לראות
ז. זפת ח. חמס ט. טהורה י. יקום כ. כרם ל. לא אוסיף עוד להכות את
כל חי כאשר עשיתי מ. מין, נ. נמרוד – He incited rebellion against
Hashem. ס. סוכה ברוח הקודש – This means she was covered
with ruach hakodesh. ע. עורב פ. פרו ורבו צ. צוהר ק. קשת
ר. ראם ש. שם ת. תרח – He was Avraham's father.

---

**ב**     תשובה comes from the word לשוב, which means to
return. One of the thirteen attributes of Hashem
is mercy. When a person sins, Hashem gives him
a chance to do תשובה, because He has mercy on
the people He created. The main steps to תשובה
are recognizing the sin, confessing to having
transgressed it, and stating that you will sincerely
try not to do the sin again.

---

**ז**     The זפת covered Moshe's תיבה only from the outside
and not from the inside. This was because the זפת
had a bad smell and Hashem did not want a צדיק
such as Moshe to be exposed to it.

---

**כ**     Wine is used to facilitate many mitzvot, such as
Kiddush, Havdala, and ברכת המזון. These are examples
of כוס של ברכה, or a cup of wine used for a mitzva.

---

**ק**     *Zocher HaBrit.*

---

Even before the Torah was given, man was expected not
to steal or murder. This was part of basic דרך ארץ. From the
time of the Creation of the world, Hashem expected man
to establish civilization based on human decency.

Questions

א. אברהם ב. ברית בין הבתרים ג. גרים ד. דמשק ה. הגר (רש״י,
16:1) ו. וינגע ז. זרעך ח. זרעך ט. ט׳ י. חוט ט. three cows, three goats, (9)
and three rams. י. ישמעאל כ. כדרלעומר ל. לוט מ. מלכיצדק
נ. נהר מצרים, נהר פרת ס. סדום ע. עצם היום פ. פרעה צ. צפונה
ק. ק׳ (100) ר. רועה צאן ש. שרי, שרה ת. תור and גוזל

---

The Jewish people are small in numbers. This ברכה demonstrates that no matter how much the nations try to persecute and destroy us, Benei Yisrael continue to flourish and develop into a great nation. The Mitzrim tried to enslave and destroy Benei Yisrael, but Hashem redeemed them from Mitzrayim. Haman tried to destroy all of the Jews in Persia, but Hashem saved them. The Nazis tried to exterminate all Jews, and even though they successfully killed many of us, they could not wipe out the entire Jewish nation.

---

A ברית מילה is performed on the eighth day after a baby boy is born, even if that day is Shabbat. The ברית מילה is made on a להכניסו בבריתו של אברהם אבינו.

The Midrash says that Avraham saw a city lit up, and he asked: "Who was responsible for lighting up this city?" It was then that Hashem began to appear to him. Perhaps this Midrash teaches us that Avraham was able to find Hashem because he took the time to ask and search for the origin of the world. Hashem reveals Himself in different ways around us; we just have to search for Him in our world, and we will find Him.

Questions

א. אלוני ממרא ב. ביקור חולים ג. גוי גדול ד. דלת ה. הגר ו. ויחבוש את חמורו ז. זריזין מקדימין למצוות ח. חמאה or חלב ט. טובות י. יצחק כ. כוכבי השמים ל. לשון מ. מאכלת נ. נער ס. סעודה ע. עמון and מואב פ. פסח צ. צנוע ק. קח נא את בנך ר. רבקה ש. שלשה אנשים ת. תחת העץ

ז. From the time we wake up in the morning we are constantly presented with opportunities to fulfill mitzvot. We begin our day by eagerly getting up from our beds in order to pray to Hashem. In the beginning of our prayers, we recite the ברכות התורה, which enable us to study Torah. This is because we are looking for any opportunity to study Torah during the day. Every function we perform presents an opportunity to fulfill a mitzva, either through a ברכה we recite or through an act we are involved in, to demonstrate our focus on Hashem.

ט. מדות טובות are positive character traits that help us behave properly and sensitize us to our surroundings. Examples of מדות טובות are kindness, giving to others, being respectful, and modesty. These attributes are important because they help us relate to each other properly, and that helps us relate to Hashem properly.

ס. One must wash his hands before eating bread. This is called נטילת ידים. It is performed with a cup that holds a רביעית of water, and we pour a רביעית of water on each hand twice. We hold the cup in our right hand while we fill up the cup, and we pour the water on our right hand first and then we pour it on our left hand. The ברכה we make, על נטילת ידים, is said before we dry our hands. We recite המוציא לחם מן הארץ on bread. One must eat a כזית of bread in order to be obligated to say ברכת המזון. ברכת המזון is a ברכה from the Torah because it says ואכלת ושבעת וברכת.

צ    The word צנוע means hidden. צניעות is a way of life that is based on modesty and privacy. A Jew tries to lead his life with צניעות because he recognizes that Hashem is the Almighty One who controls the world, and this makes a Jew feel modest in comparison. We preserve צניעות in different ways. Dressing modestly is part of צניעות. We dress modestly by covering parts of our body. We are careful to avoid haughtiness, and we are soft-spoken.

Parsha Puzzler

According to the פסוקים, Sara laughed because she doubted that she could possibly have a son at her age, and because she doubted Hashem. She was punished for demonstrating a lack of faith in Hashem.

Questions

א. אדם and חוה   ב. בכל, בן   ג. גמל   ד. דרכי   ה. ה׳   ו. ויצא יצחק לשוח בשדה   ז. זקן ביתו   ח. חברון   ט. טובות   י. ישמעאל   כ. כנען   ל. לבן מ. מערת המכפלה   נ. נערה   ס. סדר   ע. עבר   פ. פילגשים   צ. צמיד ק. קטורה – קטורת Because her actions were comforting like the. ר. רבבה   ש. שקל כסף   ת. תושב

ו    מנחה is the afternoon prayer. One can begin praying מנחה from half a variable hour after midday, and should complete מנחה by שקיעת החמה, or sunset. Once it is close to that time, one should avoid sitting down to have a meal with bread, lest he forget to pray.

Parsha Puzzler

Maarat HaMachpela is where Adam and Chava are buried. It has, therefore, been a landmark since the beginning of civilization. By burying Sara there, Avraham wanted people to understand that the civilized world should follow the path of Sara, and the rest of the forefathers and foremothers of the Jewish people who would be buried there.

Questions

א. אדון ב. בכורה ג. גוים ד. דגן ה. הלעיטני ו. ויעתר ז. זקן
ח. חרן ט. טל י. יושב אהלים כ. כ״ב (22) ל. לחם מ. מכרה כיום
את בכורתך לי נ. נביות ס. סתמום ע. עולה תמימה פ. פדן ארם
צ. ציד ק. קול ר. רחובות ש. שדה ת. תם

ט    Pesach is in the spring, which is the time for the rejuvenation of nature. This is why the prayer for טל, dew, is recited on the first day of Pesach during תפילת מוסף. Once the prayer has been said, the custom in Eretz Yisrael and for those who pray נוסח ספרד is to insert the words "מוריד הטל" into the שמונה עשרה before the paragraph of מכלכל חיים. If a person forgot to insert מוריד הטל he does not need to repeat anything and should continue on in the שמונה עשרה.

י    תלמוד תורה is a mitzva that should be done during the day and in the evening because it says והגית בו יומם ולילה. Although one should always try to learn as much Torah as possible, one fulfills the mitzva of תלמוד תורה by learning some Torah every day, in the morning and in the evening.

ר    Rechovot, Be'er Sheva, Ashdod, Ashkelon, Yerushalayim.

Parsha Puzzler

Many explanations are offered to explain why Yitzchak intended to give the ברכה to Esav. Perhaps Yitzchak felt that by offering the birthright ברכות to Esav, he would do תשובה. Some explain that Yitzchak realized that Esav was a great hunter. Yitzchak would give Esav the ברכות, and Esav would support Yaakov, who would sit and study Torah.

Questions

א. אחד עשרה ב. באר ג. גלעד ד. דודאים ה. הפעם אודה את ה'
ו. ויפגע במקום ז. זבולון ח. חלום ט. טריפה י. יפת תואר ויפת מראה
כ. כ"ד, כהונה ל. לאה מ. מחנה נ. נשיקה ס. סביב ראשו
ע. עבודה פ. פי הבאר צ. צאן ק. קטנה ר. ראובן – From the word
re'eh, which  means that Hashem saw my pain and blessed me
with a son (Leah). ש. שפחות ת. תרפים

ו    The ideal time for praying מעריב is after צאת הכוכבים,
when it is dark outside. Although one can begin
praying מעריב as early as one and one-quarter
variable hours before sunset, if he does so, he must
repeat the קריאת שמע after dark. מעריב begins with
ברכו, and one should not talk from ברכו until after
the שמונה עשרה is recited.

Parsha Puzzler

Chazal explain that this kiss was Yaakov's reaction after wit-
nessing the beauty that Hashem created in Rachel. Rashi
says that Yaakov cried because he foresaw that Rachel would
not be buried in Maarat HaMachpela together with him.
Rashi offers an alternative explanation that Yaakov was upset
that he came to marry Rachel, but he had no gifts to offer
her.

Questions

א. ארצה שעיר ב. בנימין ג. גיד הנשה ד. דינה ה. הלכה היא בידוע
שעשיו שונא ליעקב אלא שנכמרו רחמיו באותה שעה ונשקו בכל לבו
ו. ויגוע ז. זכרים ח. חלק אותם ט. טמן י. ישראל כ. כף ירכו
ל. לאה מ. מאה שמונים נ. נקודות – They demonstrate that Esav did
not kiss or embrace Yaakov wholeheartedly. ס. סוכות ע. עבד
פ. פניאל צ. צולע ק. קטנתי מכל החסדים ומכל האמת ר. רחל
ש. שלם ת. תרי"ג

**Parsha Puzzler**

Yaakov organized his families in a line, one family after another, and each family in order of importance. The hand-maids, Bilha and Zilpa, and their children, were first, followed by Leah and her children, and then Rachel and her children. This way, if Esav killed one family, the next family would survive. With regard to all of the families it says that when they introduced themselves to Esav, the mother stepped forward first, followed by the children. Yosef was concerned that Esav would desire Rachel if he saw how beautiful she was. Therefore, he stepped in front of Rachel to protect her. It appears that this was something Yosef thought of at the moment, whereas Yaakov was more concerned at the time with protecting the children.

וישב

**Questions**

א. אלומות ב. בור ג. גפן ד. דבה רעה ה. הרה ו. וישכחהו
ז. זקונים ח. חן ט. טרף טרף יוסף י. יהודה כ. כתנת פסים ל. לשון
הרע מ. מדינים נ. נער ס. סל ע. עיניה פ. פוטיפר צ. צדקה ממני
ק. קנאה ר. ראובן ש. שכם ת. תמר

| ו | Many empires persecuted and tried to destroy Benei Yisrael, and even though they successfully killed many Jews, Hashem saved the nation. The establishment of the State of Israel and its survival is also reason to have more בטחון in Hashem. There are many different people in the Torah and many rabbis who demonstrate בטחון in Hashem. Many times people we know teach us בטחון by the way they behave and the faith they have in Hashem. |

| ל | לשון הרע is when a person speaks negatively about someone else. רכילות is when a person goes to someone and tells him or her things they heard about a third person. Some people think that if they are telling the truth they are allowed to talk about |

other people, but this is not so. Even if the things that are said are true or said as a joke, it is still considered לשון הרע or רכילות. If we keep our mouths busy with positive things such as תפילה, Torah, and learning, we will have less time to speak wrongly.

From the פסוקים, it appears that Yaakov was wrong for favoring Yosef. However, this does not excuse what the brothers did to Yosef.

א. אסנת ב. בריאות ג. גביע ד. דלות ה. האיש ו. ויתנכר ז. זהב ח. חלומות ט. טובות י. יהודה כ. כסף ל. לכו אל יוסף אשר יאמר לכם תעשו מ. מנשה נ. נכמרו רחמיו ס. סימן ע. עבד פ. פותר צ. צפנת פענח ק. קשות ר. רעב ש. שמעון ת. תשמע

Chazal explain that Yosef wanted his brothers to be accused of stealing, just like they had "stolen" Yaakov's heart when he thought Yosef had been killed. Yosef wanted to put his brothers through difficulties, so that they would feel the pain they had caused him. This way they would sincerely know how Yosef felt when he was sold into slavery, and that would enable them to experience sincere תשובה.

א. אסון ב. בושה ג. גושן ד. דברו אחיו אתו ה. העוד אבי חי ו. וינשק ז. זבחים ח. חליפות שמלות ט. טף י. יהודה כ. כסף ל. לוי מ. מקדש, משכן נ. נילוס ס. סכנה ע. עגלות פ. פוטיפרע צ. צואר ק. קריאת שמע ר. רכוש ש. שבעים ת. תרגזו

ב    The Gemara in Tractate Bava Metzia says that one who embarrasses his friend is considered as if he has "spilled his friend's blood," i.e., as if he has killed him. This is because when you embarrass someone

ב in public they are so humiliated that they'd rather be away from everyone, as if they were dead. The Gemara also declares that one who embarrasses his friend will not be rewarded a portion in the World to Come.

מ There are three fast days which connect to the destruction of the Beit HaMikdash. Asara BeTevet, the tenth of the month of Tevet, was the day that Nevuchadnetzar surrounded Yerushalayim to lay siege on the city. This was the beginning of the חורבן. The seventeenth of the month of Tammuz, Shiva Asar BeTammuz was the day that the walls of Yerushalayim were broken into. On the ninth of Av, Tisha B'Av, both the first and the second Beit HaMikdash were destroyed. Two causes of the חורבן mentioned in the Gemara are that people did not respect one another and that they disgraced the תלמידי חכמים. We can rectify these mistakes by being sensitive to one another and respecting our rabbis properly.

ק One is obligated to recite קריאת שמע in the morning and at night. The first פסוק of קריאת שמע is "שמע ישראל, etc.," which is the way a person accepts Hashem and the responsibility of keeping the mitzvot. When one says קריאת שמע, he should concentrate on the fact that Hashem is the sole Creator of the universe. One should also be careful to say every single letter of קריאת שמע clearly, especially when the last letter of one word is the same as the first letter of the next word. For example, with the words בכל לבבך, one should be careful to pause in between the two words, so that the *lamed*s do not cause the two words to sound like one.

The first thing Pharaoh asked Yaakov was, "כמה ימי, etc.," which means "How old are you?" Yaakov responded, "מעט ורעים, etc." Yaakov complained that his life was short and difficult. Rashi explains that Hashem punished Yaakov by shortening his life because he complained. Even if a person experiences difficulties, one must always be thankful and appreciative to be alive.

ויחי

א. אחרית הימים ב. בכורו שוו הדר לו ג. גדעון ד. דן ה. המלאך הגואל ו. וידגו לרוב ז. זבולון – To demonstrate that even though he did not sit and learn like Yissachar, since he supported his brother to learn, he is considered just as important and was blessed first. ח. חמור ט. טוב י. יד ימינו, יהושע כ. כתר ל. לא יסור שבט מיהודה מ. מאה שלשים ושבע נ. נאסף אל עמי ס. סופה להיות עפרה כנים ע. עצמות פ. פדן ארם צ. צאן ק. קרח ר. ראש ש. שיכל ידיו ת. תוכחה

> **ה**
> One should not talk or eat after reciting קריאת שמע על המיטה. By reciting קריאת שמע על המיטה, we ask Hashem to protect us during the night when we are sleeping. One does not recite קריאת שמע על המיטה on the first night of Pesach, because it is referred to in the Torah as ליל שימורים, the night that Hashem assured Benei Yisrael of protection.

The Torah records how many years צדיקים lived in order to demonstrate that they were worthy to live a long life because of their righteousness. Rashi explains that Yaakov made Yosef swear to bury him in Maarat HaMachpela because, as a leader in Mitzrayim, Yosef was the only one of the brothers who had the authority to make it happen.

Questions

א. אחים ב. ברית מילה ג. גרשון ד. דתן ואבירם ה. הבה נתחכמה לו
ו. והן לא יאמינו לי ולא ישמעו בקולי ז. זפת ח. חותן, חתן ט. טוב
י. יוכבד ומרים כ. כבד פה וכבד לשון ל. לוי מ. מילדות נ. נחש ס. סנה
ע. עמרם פ. פניו צ. צרעת ק. קדוש ר. רעואל ש. שלשה ירחים
ת. תבן

**פ** When praying, one has to show respect to Hashem by concentrating on the words he is saying. In order to do this, one can either look into the siddur or close his or her eyes. When we close our eyes, we cannot see anything else that may distract us from what we are saying. The most important parts of תפילה that require כוונה, proper intentions, are קריאת שמע, particularly the first פסוק, and שמונה עשרה, particularly the first ברכה. One should close his or her eyes and avoid looking directly at the Kohanim during ברכת כהנים.

**ק** In the Beit HaMikdash, everyone was required to walk barefoot so as not to have any separation between their feet and the floor. This connected people to the קדושה of the Mikdash. The Kohanim who worked in the Mikdash did so barefoot. Today, the Kohanim must have a separation between their feet and the floor, because we are not allowed to imitate the way things were done in the Beit HaMikdash.

Parsha Puzzler

Moshe was concerned that Benei Yisrael were not yet worthy to leave Mitzrayim. He did not want to get their hopes up, only to let them down, because of these concerns. Hashem punished Moshe for his poor judgment of Benei Yisrael by giving him צרעת on his arm. A simpler explanation is that Moshe hesitated out of his own modesty. Moshe still felt unworthy to lead Benei Yisrael out of Mitzrayim, even though Hashem had approached him to do so. Hashem wanted Moshe to understand that modesty is important, but not when it interferes with one's duties, such as leading the Jewish people.

Questions

א. אלישבע  ב. ברד  ג. גרשון, קהת, ומררי  ד. דודה  ה. הוא אהרן ומשה  ו. ויוסף לחטוא ויכבד לבו  ז. זבחים  ח. חול  ט. טרם  י. יד חזקה  כ. כנים  ל. לי לעם  מ. מורשה  נ. נחשון  ס. סבלות  ע. ערל שפתים  פ. פנחס  צ. צפרדע  ק. קוצר רוח ועבודה קשה  ר. ראובן, שמעון, ולוי  ש. שמונים, שמונים ושלוש  ת. תנור

> **ח** הכרת הטוב means to recognize the good and to be grateful for the good that is done for you. Hashem created Chava for Adam because He did not want Adam to be lonely. This was a gift from Hashem to Adam. Yet, after Adam ate from the tree of knowledge, and Hashem approached him, he immediately blamed his sin on Chava. By doing so, Adam was ungrateful to Hashem.

> **מ** A ירושה is an inheritance, and a מתנה is a gift. An inheritance belongs to someone because it is rightfully his or hers, but a gift is given to someone although it did not rightfully belong to the person beforehand. Eretz Yisrael is a ירושה, an inheritance, because it has rightfully belonged to Benei Yisrael from the beginning of time.

> **צ** Avraham Avinu was מוסר נפש when he was thrown into כבשן האש, the fire, because he believed in Hashem. Rabbi Akiva was מוסר נפש when he taught Torah to his students, even when the Romans said that anyone who did so would be killed. The

Rambam was מוסר נפש when he studied Torah in Spain, regardless of the fact that the Almohads proclaimed it punishable by death. During World War II, the partisans were מוסר נפש in order to fight the Nazis and free Jews from the death camps. In our generation, the Israeli soldiers are מוסר נפש protecting the country for the sake of the Jewish people.

**Parsha Puzzler**

There are many different explanations offered to this difficult problem. Rashi explains that Pharaoh had free choice at the beginning, but when Hashem saw how cruel and stubborn he was, he punished him by hardening his heart. Hashem used Pharaoh as an example to others for what happens to someone who is cruel and ignores His command. Nevertheless, this remains a difficult question that has been argued and discussed by many commentators.

בא

**Questions**

א. ארבה ב. בכור ג. גר ד. דם ה. החודש הזה לכם ו. והגדת לבנך
ז. זבח פסח ח. חושך ט. טובל בדם י. יראה כ. כבש ל. לילה
מ. מזוזה נ. נותר ס. ספות כסף ע. עשב פ. פדיון הבן צ. צלי אש
ק. קידוש החודש ר. רשע ש. שבע ת. תושב

ה  קידוש החודש is the establishment of a new month. When there was a Sanhedrin, a Jewish high court of law, this mitzva was done through the testimony of two witnesses. The witnesses saw the new moon and traveled to the Sanhedrin in Yerushalayim to describe what they saw. The Sanhedrin interrogated the witnesses, and if they accepted their testimony, they declared a new month. Today we do not have a Sanhedrin, but we continue to establish the new month through a lunar calendar designed by Hillel in the time of the Mishna. We commemorate what the Sanhedrin did by saying a special תפילה, called ברכת החודש, on the Shabbat before Rosh Chodesh, the new month. The twelve Jewish months are Tishrei, Cheshvan, Kislev, Tevet, Shvat, Adar, Nisan, Iyar, Sivan, Tammuz, Av, and Elul. Beginning at least three days after the מולד, the beginning of the new moon, we say the תפילה called קידוש לבנה, sanctifying the new moon. קידוש לבנה can be said up until the tenth day after the מולד. It is preferable to recite קידוש לבנה with a *minyan* and on Motzaei Shabbat, Saturday night, when people are dressed respectfully, in Shabbat clothing. One should also preferably say קידוש לבנה under the sky and not under a roof or covering.

מ    The mezuza is a parchment with the first chapter of קריאת שמע written on it. One places it on the right side of the doorpost as he or she enters a room. It is customary to kiss the mezuza as one passes through the doorway.

פ    The mitzva of פדיון הבן is required when a firstborn son is born to a Yisrael mother and father. The father must redeem the child by giving money to a Kohen as a gift. The פדיון הבן cannot be done until thirty days after the son is born, and should be done right away on the thirty-first day.

ש    חמץ is anything made from grain (or derivatives of the grain) that was left in water for enough time to rise. Prior to Pesach, someone is appointed (usually the rabbi of a community) to sell people's חמץ to a non-Jew. This is called מכירת חמץ and is done to ensure that any חמץ we may not be aware of owning no longer belongs to us. On the night before Pesach, one must search the house with a candle and check

if there is any חמץ around. This is the mitzva of בדיקת
חמץ. On the next morning, Erev Pesach, one burns any
leftover חמץ in preparation for Pesach, and declares
all חמץ as nothing. This mitzva is called ביעור חמץ.

Hashem did certain miracles בעצם היום, in the middle of the
day, in order to demonstrate to the world the miraculous
events that He does for Benei Yisrael. קריעת ים סוף, יציאת מצרים,
מתן תורה, and the מבול in the time of Noach were all done
בעצם היום.

א. אז ישיר  ב. ביבשה  ג. גאה גאה  ד. דרך ארץ פלשתים  ה. השבע
השביע  ו. והיה כאשר ירים משה ידו וגבר ישראל וכאשר יניח ידו וגבר
עמלק  ז. זרע גד  ח. חור  ט. טל  י. ימין  כ. כלב  ל. לחם משנה
מ. מרים  נ. נטה את ידך על הים  ס. סוכות  ע. ענני הכבוד  פ. פחד
צ. צפיחית בדבש  ק. קריעת ים סוף  ר. רפידים  ש. שבת שירה  ת. תומך

א | אז ישיר is found in the first section of תפילת שחרית
called פסוקי דזמרא, which is a collection of תפילות that
praise the greatness of Hashem. אז ישיר is part of פסוקי
דזמרא because it is the song that Benei Yisrael sang to
Hashem, praising Him for saving them miraculously
by splitting the ים סוף. פסוקי דזמרא opens with a ברכה
called ברוך שאמר and closes with the ברכה of ישתבח.
Therefore, one should not talk from the start of פסוקי
דזמרא until the end, unless it is conversation related
to the halachot of תפילה.

Benei Yisrael were told to look up at the hands of Moshe in
order to prevail over Amalek, but it was not Moshe's hands
that saved them. Moshe's hands were raised to remind
Benei Yisrael to look heavenward and remember that their
lives were dependent on their faith in Hashem. It was the
faith that Benei Yisrael had in Hashem that saved them, not
Moshe's hands.

א. **אנכי ה׳ אלקיך**　ב. **בית יעקב** – Because the women are responsible for the continuity of the Jewish people by educating Jewish children from the home.　ג. גזית　ד. דיין　ה. הר　ו. ויחן ישראל　ז. זכור את יום השבת לקדשו　ח. חזק　ט. טהור　י. יתרו　כ. כבד את אביך ואת אמך　ל. לא תרצח, לא תנאף, לא תגנוב, לא תענה ברעך עד שקר, לא תחמוד　מ. ממלכת כהנים　נ. נעשה　ס. סיני　ע. ענן כבד　פ. פוטיאל　צ. צפורה　ק. קדוש　ר. ראשים　ש. שמלתם　ת. תורה

ב　Women are obligated in all of the מצוות לא תעשה, prohibitions from the Torah. Women are only obligated in the מצוות עשה, the positive mitzvot, which are not time bound. One of the reasons why this is so is because men tend to be more involved in the material world and therefore require more daily guidance. Therefore, they must keep the time bound mitzvot, which assist them to remain spiritual in more challenging situations.

ו　Benei Yisrael are always stronger when they are united. When Benei Yisrael were preparing to conquer Eretz Yisrael, Reuven and Gad approached Moshe and told him they wanted to settle in the Jordan valley and not in Eretz Yisrael. Moshe accepted their request, provided that first they would unite with all of the tribes to conquer Eretz Yisrael together. During the reign of Shlomo HaMelech, Benei Yisrael were united, the Beit HaMikdash was built, and Eretz Yisrael thrived. During the reign of Rechavam, Benei Yisrael split into the kingdoms of Yehuda and Yisrael and many people worshiped עבודה זרה. One of the reasons the Beit HaMikdash was destroyed was because of the lack of respect and lack of unity within Benei Yisrael. We have to learn tolerance and patience in order to encourage unity among us.

ז  It is a mitzva from the Torah to commemorate the Shabbat. We fulfill this mitzva by saying the Kiddush on wine. הדלקת נרות, lighting the Shabbat candles, is a מצוה מדרבנ, given to us by the rabbis. עונג שבת means to have a nice meal on Shabbat and is also a מצוה מדרבנ. There are certain practices we do on Shabbat that are not mitzvot, but they enhance רוח שבת, the spirit of Shabbat. These include singing זמירות שבת, songs at the Shabbat table, and having extra special delicacies to eat.

כ  The Gemara says that one must make sure that their parents have food, clothing, and shoes. One must open the door for a parent and allow them to enter or exit a room first. Even though the Gemara offers clear guidelines on how to fulfill this mitzva, respecting parents remains a very difficult mitzva to do because we are with them a lot of the time, and as a result we may take them and the relationship we have with them for granted.

Parsha Puzzler

The Gemara explains that the mitzva of Shabbat was given before כיבוד אב ואם to demonstrate that even though respecting parents is important, listening to Hashem comes first. If a parent tells a child to desecrate Shabbat (or to ignore any mitzva in the Torah), they are not allowed to listen to their parents, because obeying Hashem is more important.

משפטים

Questions

א.אמה ב.ביכורים ג.גר ד.דלת ה.השבתאבידה ו.ואלההמשפטים– This connects all of the mitzvot of the parsha to the Ten Commandments in the previous parsha and demonstrates that all the mitzvot are from Sinai. ז. זמירה ח. חרישה ט. טרפה י. יתום כ. כפל ל. לא תבשל גדי בחלב אמו מ. מדבר שקר תרחק נ. נדב ואביהו ס. סקילה ע. עבד עברי פ. פלישתים צ. צדיק ק. קציר ר. רפא ירפא ש. שבעת המינים ת. תשים לפניהם

ב     The שבעת המינים are wheat, barley, grapes (wine), figs, pomegranates, olives, and dates. The ברכה אחרונה on products made of wheat or barley such as bread, is ברכת המזון. On cake or crackers made from wheat or barley the ברכה אחרונה is על המחיה, or מעין שלש. The ברכה אחרונה on wine is על הגפן, or מעין שלש, and on the rest of the fruits it is על העץ, or מעין שלש. If one were going to eat from all of the שבעת המינים, he or she would first say the ברכה of בורא מיני מזונות on the wheat (which would also cover the barley), then the ברכה of בורא פרי הגפן on the wine, and finally, the ברכה of בורא פרי העץ on the olives (having in mind the rest of the fruit; this ברכה would cover the rest of the fruit). If there were grapes instead of wine, then one would make the ברכה of בורא פרי העץ on the olives and have in mind the rest of the fruit.

ה     The general rule is that if there is a סימן (identifiable sign) on the lost object, then one is obligated to try to return it. The person who claims the object must identify the סימן to prove that it is his. If one finds an item in a public place without a סימן then he or she can keep it. There is no clear way to establish whom it belongs to, as there is no clear סימן. Moreover, since it was lost in a public place, it is assumed that the owner has given up hope of finding what he lost.

ז, ח     During the שמיטה year, one cannot work his field. This demonstrates faith in Hashem, and our belief that all produce and crops are ultimately the result of His ברכות. Today, we also refrain from working the land during the שמיטה year, and according to most opinions, the mitzva of שמיטה today is a מצוה מדרבנן.

ל In a kosher home, to separate between meat and milk we have separate sets of dishes, separate countertops, and many people have separate cupboards and sinks. There are different customs regarding waiting between meat and milk. Some people wait one hour, some wait three hours, and some wait into the sixth hour. The most popular and most accepted custom is to wait six hours. If one eats milk products and wants to eat meat, he must first wipe and rinse out his mouth. This process is called קינוח and הדחה. Brushing teeth is an acceptable way to fulfill this requirement.

**Parsha Puzzler**

משפטים are mitzvot that we generally understand the reason for. חוקים are mitzvot that are not understood. The mitzva of פרה אדומה, burning a red cow and sprinkling its ashes on a person who has become טמא through contact with a corpse, is an example of a חוק.

תרומה

**Questions**

א. אבני מילואים, אבני שוהם ב. בשמים ג. גבעים ד. דיבר ה. הפרשה ו. ווים ועמודים ז. זר ח. חלוון ט. טבעות י. יריעות כ. כרובים ל. לולאות מ. מנורה נ. נחושת ס. סוככים ע. עצי שטים פ. פעמותיו צ. צפון ק. קרשים ר. רבוע ש. שמן זית זך ת. תחש

ה The most popular way to give צדקה is by giving poor people money, but there are many other ways to fulfill this mitzva. One can provide poor people with clothing, food, or services. The best form of צדקה is providing someone with a job. It is also preferable to give צדקה anonymously, and to avoid revealing where the צדקה came from. This way the poor person does not get embarrassed that he is receiving help from others.

**Parsha Puzzler**

The commentators explain that any synagogue or *beit midrash* where there is תפילה or Torah learning is called a Mikdash. This פסוק was written in the plural to demonstrate that Hashem dwells anywhere that Jews pray or study Torah and not only in the Mishkan itself.

תצוה

**Questions**

א. אדום ב. בקר, בין הערבים ג. גג ד. דם ה. הדיוט ו. ואתה, משה ז. זרה ח. חרש ט. טורים י. יד, ידיים כ. כתפות ל. לב אהרן מ. מעיל נ. נזר ס. סמיכה ע. עולת תמיד פ. פעמונים צ. ציץ ק. קטורת ר. ריח ניחוח ש. שמונה ת. תמיד

**Parsha Puzzler**

The Gemara in Tractate Yoma says that the כתונת (shirt) atoned for murder, the מכנסיים (pants) atoned for promiscuity, the מצנפת (hat) atoned for haughtiness, the אבנט (sash) atoned for bad feelings in the heart, the חושן (breastplate) atoned for bad judgment, the אפוד (apron-like garment) atoned for idolatry, the מעיל (cloak) atoned for לשון הרע, and the ציץ (headband) atoned for stubbornness.

כי תישא

א. אות ב. בצלאל ג. גדול ד. דל ה. הראני נא את כבדך ו. ונקה ז. ז' סיון ח. חטא העגל ט. טהור י. י"ז תמוז כ. כיור ל. לוי מ. מי לה' אלי, מתתיהו נ. נזמים, נשים ס. סרו מהר מן הדרך ע. עם קשה עורף פ. פנים אל פנים צ. (ל)צחק ק. קרני אור ר. רחום ש. שלש ת. תרומה

> א We prepare for Shabbat in a special way: we bathe, dress in nice clothing, and prepare delicacies and special food for the Shabbat meals. We spend extra time praying and learning Torah on Shabbat. We also make Kiddush on wine and eat סעודות שבת, the three special meals on Shabbat that involve delicious food and זמירות שבת. To preserve the spirit of Shabbat, we avoid talking about weekday matters and discussing business transactions, and we refrain from doing weekday activities such as sports and exercise.

Hashem wanted all the Jewish people to know that they are equal and that they must unite. Therefore, everyone was instructed to give the same amount, a half shekel, which required another person's half shekel in order to make it whole.

א. אהליאב ב. בצלאל ג. גביעים ד. דיבור ה. הר, הכיפורים ו. ו'
(6) ז. זהב ח. חכם לב ט. טוויה י. יעים כ. כסף ל. לא תבערו אש
מ. מראות נ. נשיאים ס. סביב ע. עדת בני ישראל פ. פרחים
צ. צלעותיו, צדיו ק. קרן ר. רוקח, רוקם ש. שמן המשחה, שמן למאור
ת. תכלת

*Parshat Teruma* offers a general description of the construction of the Mishkan while here in *Parshat Vayak'hel* the Torah offers detailed instructions regarding the Mishkan and its utensils. Rav Shlomo Aviner suggests that this demonstrates the importance of learning to focus on the fine details, which are so important in *halacha*.

א. איתמר ב. בין אהל מועד ובין המזבח ג. גבלות ד. דרך קשירה, ד'
חוטין ה. הקודש ו. ויהי נעם ז. זרת ח. חושב ט. טהורה י. ידים
כ. כלים ל. לא יקרע מ. משכן – The two words refer to the two Batei HaMikdash that would be destroyed because of Benei Yisrael's sins. נ. נגבה ס. סכת ע. ענן פ. פתוחי חותם צ. ציץ ק. קודש
ר. רימונים ש. שרשרת ת. תחש

> In the time of the Beit HaMikdash, the Kohanim had to remain in a state of purity. In order to accomplish this, they had to constantly wash their hands to ensure that whatever they would handle or touch would stay pure. A Kohen could eat תרומה, a gift of food given to the Kohanim, only in a state of purity. Even though today there is no Beit HaMikdash and

we are unable to preserve purity, we wash our hands
before we eat bread to maintain practices done in
the Beit HaMikdash. This is referred to as סרך תרומה.
The Levi'im wash the hands of the Kohanim before
ברכת כהנים, the blessing of the Kohanim. Their hands
should be washed up to the beginning of the wrist.

Rav Shlomo Aviner explains that this teaches us that every
detail in Judaism is important. One may think that some
mitzvot are minor or that some rabbinic requirements are
superfluous. The Torah mentions every detail of the Mishkan to teach us that just like one has to be careful about every
detail in order to construct a Mishkan, so too, one must pay
attention to every detail of *halacha* and Jewish tradition in
order to construct a Jewish home.

ויקרא

א. אדם ב. בקר ג. גיד הנשה ד. דם ה. הפשטה ו. ואשם והשיב את
הגזילה אשר גזל ז. זריקה ח. חטאת ט. טמאת י. (בני) יונה כ. כליות
ל. לשון חיבה ולשון שמלאכי השרת משתמשים בו מ. מבין הכרובים
נ. נשמה – This word, soul, is used to demonstrate that when a
poor person brings a *korban mincha* he shows such dedication
that Hashem says that it is as if he is willing to sacrifice his soul.
ס. סמיכה ע. (מנחת) עני פ. פתות אותה פתים צ. צאן ק. קודש ר. ריח
ניחוח ש. שבע ת. תמים

ג    Certain parts of the animal are not kosher, such as
the fat of and by the tail, the fat on the kidneys, the
muscle that surrounds the sciatic nerve, and the
blood that was in veins or arteries at the time of
death. Kidneys are generally considered non-kosher,
as there is no way to get all the blood, which is not
kosher, out of them.

ח Our תפילה, or prayers, today replace the קרבנות offered in the Beit HaMikdash. In parts of our תפילה, we ask Hashem to restore the Beit HaMikdash so that we can once again serve Him and offer קרבנות. One of these תפילות is the ברכה of רצה in the שמונה עשרה.

**Parsha Puzzler**

The word קרבן comes from the root word קרב, to be close. One of the explanations given to this question is that we would be willing to sacrifice ourselves for Hashem; however, we continue to live for the sake of getting closer to Him. The animal is offered on the מזבח in place of man.

צו

**Questions**

א. אש ב. בוקר ג. גדול ד. דרך ארץ ה. הקהל ו. ויעש אהרן ובניו את כל הדברים אשר צוה ה' ביד משה ז. זריזות ח. חלב ט. טהור י. ימין כ. כרת ל. לזכרון מ. מחבת נ. נותר ס. סולת ע. וערך עליה העולה והקטיר עליה חלבי השלמים פ. פיגול צ. ציץ ק. קמיצה ר. רקיק ש. שני ת. תודה

ב שחרית is the morning prayer which corresponds to the תמיד של שחר, morning sacrifice, offered in the Beit HaMikdash. One can pray שחרית (שמונה עשרה) from נץ החמה, the first ray of sunlight in the sky, which is a special mitzva called *vatikin*. One should preferably finish praying שחרית by the end of four variable hours into the day. One must finish praying שחרית by חצות היום, midday. Once there is light in the sky, one should refrain from doing anything until praying שחרית.

ד דרך ארץ means "the way of the land" and is the basic concept that guides people to behave properly. דרך ארץ teaches us to have manners and to conduct ourselves with positive character traits, מידות טובות, that help us behave properly and sensitize us to our surroundings. Examples of מידות טובות are kindness, modesty, giving to others, and being respectful. These attributes are so important because they help us relate to each other properly, and that helps us relate to Hashem properly as well.

ז  זריזות means to be eager and earnest. When it comes to performing mitzvot we should always be eager to do so and respond immediately. For example, when we are given an opportunity to give צדקה, we should do so right away; or when we have the opportunity to help someone, we should do so quickly.

ת  The ברכה that is recited if one experienced a miracle is "שעשה לי נס במקום הזה." One makes this ברכה when he passes by a place where he experienced a miracle.

A קרבן עולה is offered by a person who intentionally sinned, but the Torah does not specify his punishment, or by someone who did not perform a positive mitzva. One can also offer an עולה in order to raise his spirituality. This קרבן is totally consumed by the מזבח, and no one eats from it. A קרבן שלמים is offered by anyone who wants to show their love for Hashem and their recognition of His greatness. Part of the קרבן שלמים is consumed on the מזבח, part of it is eaten by the Kohen, and part of it is eaten by the owner of the animal.

שמיני

א. אהרן ובניו  ב. בלולה בשמן  ג. גמל  ד. דאה דוכיפת  ה. הורו הלכה בפני משה רבם  ו. והתקדישתם והייתם קדושים כי קדוש אני  ז. זרה  ח. חרס  ט. טמא, טהור  י. יין  כ. כי קדוש אני  ל. להבדיל בין הקודש ובין החול ובין הטמא ובין הטהור  מ. מפרסת פרסה  נ. נוגע, נבילה  ס. סנפיר  ע. ערב  פ. פתח אהל מועד  צ. צרעה  ק. קשקשת  ר. ראש חודש  ש. שוסעת שסע  ת. תפרעו, תפרומו

ג  A kosher animal must have split hooves and chew its cud. A horse and a rabbit are not kosher because they do not have split hooves. A dog is not kosher because it does not have split hooves and it does not chew its cud.

ד  The Torah lists all kosher and non-kosher birds. Generally speaking, birds of prey are not kosher.

י  One is not allowed to drink wine before praying to ensure that his mind is clear during תפילה and to allow him to concentrate on the meaning of the words. Wine is associated with joy and happiness. Therefore, during the nine days of mourning prior to Tisha B'Av, one also refrains from drinking wine. On Purim, it is a mitzva to drink wine during the סעודה, the meal in which we celebrate the miraculous way Hashem saved Benei Yisrael from Haman's decree.

ק  The swordfish has fins, but it is not kosher because it does not have scales. Shellfish are not kosher because they do not have scales or fins.

The Torah lists only one animal, the pig, of all the thousands of animals in the world that have split hooves but do not chew their cud. Only Hashem could know this fact at the time the Torah was given. This helps demonstrate the authenticity of the Torah from Hashem.

תזריע–מצורע

א. אשה ב. בן יונה ג. גיבח ד. דל ה. הפך לבן ו. ושרף את הבגד
ז. זכר ח. חטאת ט. טח את הבית י. ירקרקות כ. כהן ל. לשון הרע
מ. מחוץ למחנה נ. נגע ס. ספחת ע. עולה פ. פשה צ. ציפורים
ק. קודש ר. ראש, רגליו ש. שבוע, שבועיים ת. תורת המצורע

ל **לשון הרע** is when one says negative things about another. Some people think that if what they say is the truth, they are allowed to talk about the person, but this is not so. Even if the things that are said are true or a joke, they are still considered לשון הרע. If we keep our mouths busy with positive things such as תפילה and Torah study, we will have less time to speak wrongly.

A person gets צרעת because he spoke לשון הרע. Therefore, it is appropriate that the Kohen has to proclaim that he is טהור, using his speech, which reminds the מצורע of why he was inflicted with צרעת in the first place.

אחרי מות

א. איש ב. בעדו ובעד ביתו ג. גורל ד. דקה מן הדקה ה. האזרח
והגר הגר בתוככם ו. וחי בהם ז. זריזות ח. חדש השביעי בעשור לחדש
ט. טובל י. יחשב כ. כרת ל. לכפר מ. מולך נ. נבילה ס. סמים
ע. עפר פ. פשע צ. ציד חיה או עוף ק. קדש הקדשים ר. ראשו
ש. שוחט, שופך דמים ת. תענו את נפשתיכם

ב These are the ten days beginning with Rosh HaShana and concluding with Yom Kippur, during which one is supposed to be concerned primarily with doing תשובה. The Gemara explains that there are basically three steps to תשובה: חרטה – remorse, וידוי – confession, and קבלה לעתיד – accepting upon himself that in the future he will not sin again.

ו There are 248 positive commandments, which are called מצוות עשה and 365 negative commandments or prohibitions, which are called מצוות לא תעשה.

ט A מקוה is a body of water that has not been poured but is from a pure source such as direct rainwater, the ocean, or rivers or streams. The measurement for a kosher מקוה is forty *se'ah* of pure water.

ת   Some of the functions we must refrain from on Yom
Kippur are eating and drinking, bathing, rubbing
ourselves with oil, and wearing leather shoes.

The Gemara explains: אין קטיגור נעשה סניגור, "A prosecutor
cannot serve as a defender." If the Kohen Gadol would wear
gold, it would remind Hashem of the עגל הזהב, when Benei
Yisrael worshiped idolatry. On Yom Kippur, the Day of
Atonement, we do not want the Kohen Gadol, our defender,
to serve as a prosecutor.

קדושים

א. איש אביו ואמו תיראו, אלילים   ב. בצדק תשפט עמיתיך   ג. גר, גרים
הייתם במצרים   ד. דן לכף זכות   ה. הוכח תוכיח   ו. ואהבת לרעך כמוך
ז. זבת חלב ודבש   ח. חרש   ט. טובע בים   י. ירגמו   כ. כלאים
ל. לא תנקום ולא תנטור   מ. מולך   נ. נאמן לשלם שכר   ס. סופך לכחש,
סופך לשקר, סופך לישבע לשקר   ע. עורלה   פ. פאה   צ. צמר, פשתים
ק. קדושים תהיו – To separate oneself from promiscuity, but to
behave modestly.   ר. רוכל   ש. שיבה   ת. (לא) תגנבו, (לא) תשנא את
אחיך בלבבך, (לא) תשקרו איש בעמיתו, (לא) תשבעו בשמי לשקר Not to
steal, not to hate someone, not to lie, not to swear falsely in the
name of Hashem.

ד   Sometimes people assume wrongly that others are
talking about them. This is not fair. דן לכף זכות teaches
us to see people in a positive light and to judge them
favorably.

פ, צ   One cannot wear שעטנז, garments of wool and flax
together, even to try the garments on for a short
period. It is permissible to try clothing on if there is a
doubt whether there is שעטנז in the clothing. In order
to avoid שעטנז, one brings clothing (particularly suits
or expensive clothing) to a שעטנז laboratory, where
they inspect the clothing under a microscope for שעטנז.

ר. לשון הרע is when a person speaks negatively about someone else. רכילות is when a person goes to someone and tells him or her things they heard about a third person.

ש. A person is a שיבה, an elderly person who deserves respect, from the age of seventy. Once a שיבה is within 4 אמות (about 6 feet) of you, you must stand for him and remain standing until he passes by. This could commonly occur on a bus when you are sitting and an elderly person enters the bus; you should stand and offer the שיבה your seat.

The Ramban explains that קדושה means to control even the things that are permissible to us. It is permissible for a person to eat and drink, but certainly that is not what we should be doing all day. קדושים תהיו is a direction and a way of guiding our lives properly.

אמור

א. אלמנה ב. בת כהן ג. גרושה ד. דבר יום ביומו ה. הושבתי – This means to be seated, which means that Hashem placed Benei Yisrael on the clouds. ו. ולקחתם ביום הראשון ז. זכרון ח. חלל ט. טמא י. יום הכיפורים כ. כסות נקיה ל. למען ידעו דורותיכם כי בסוכות הושבתי את בני ישראל מ. מת מצוה נ. נדר, נדבה ס. ספירת העומר ע. ענני הכבוד פ. פרי עץ הדר צ. צאן ק. קודש ר. ראשו לא יפרע ובגדיו לא יפרם, ראש ש. שאר ת. תשרי

ד. When one misses a certain תפילה, one can do תשלומין, make up for the תפילה missed. One does so by saying an extra שמונה עשרה at the following תפילה. For example, if one missed שחרית, then at מנחה he would pray the שמונה עשרה a second time. The first

ד   שמונה עשרה is for מנחה and the second one is for שחרית. One should pause a few seconds between each שמונה עשרה and have in mind during the second one that it is to make up for the שחרית that was missed. One can do תשלומין only with the prayer that follows, but not after that.

כ   The Gemara learns, based on a פסוק in the book of *Yeshayahu*, that it is proper to have special clothing for Shabbat. If a person does not have a change of clothing then he should clean and iron his garment for the sake of Shabbat. It is also preferable to have special shoes for Shabbat; however, if he does not have a change of shoes he should clean his everyday shoes for the sake of Shabbat.

ל   According to Rabbi Eliezer in the Gemara in Tractate Sukka, the sukka reminds us of the ענני הכבוד, the clouds that surrounded the camp of Benei Yisrael in the מדבר. The sukka surrounds us and serves as our shelter. Much like the ענני הכבוד, when one sits in the sukka he should feel as if he is surrounded by the presence of Hashem.

נ   If one makes a נדר, a vow, then he must fulfill it in order to avoid making a false oath. If it is impossible to fulfill the נדר, then he must do התרת נדרים, nullifying the נדר. It is customary to do התרת נדרים before Rosh HaShana in order to rid oneself of any oaths taken prior to the new year. התרת נדרים involves going in front of a בית דין, which can be made up of three men above the age of thirteen, and asking them to nullify the נדר with a special text found in the siddur.

ס  ספירת העומר, the counting of the *Omer*, lasts forty-nine days. It begins on the second night of Pesach and concludes the night before Shavuot. Every night after צאת הכוכבים, nightfall, one should make the ברכה of על ספירת העומר, and then count the day. For example, the first day one would recite the ברכה, and then count, "היום יום אחד לעומר." One can count the entire evening. If he forgets to count in the evening, then he can count the entire next day without a ברכה and continue the following evening with a ברכה. However, if he forgets to count the entire day, then he should count the day, but he can no longer recite the ברכה during the rest of the Omer period.

פ  An etrog has to be whole, without any part of it bitten off or missing. It is a הידור מצוה, beautifying the mitzva, if one tries to get a beautiful etrog that is yellow and shaped nicely.

*Parsha Puzzler*

A Kohen Gadol is not allowed to marry a divorced woman or a widow. A Kohen Hedyot is not permitted to marry a divorced woman but he is permitted to marry a widow with children. The Kohen Gadol can come in contact and become טמא only for a מת מצוה, a corpse that is not being taken care of for burial by anyone, whereas the Kohen Hedyot can become טמא for seven close relatives as well. A Kohen Gadol has eight special garments that he wears while performing עבודה in the Mikdash, whereas the Kohen Hedyot has only four garments.

בהר

*Questions*

א. אדמה  ב. באר היטב  ג. גואל  ד. דרור  ה. הוגנת  ו. וישבתם על הארץ לבטח  ז. זמירה or זריעה  ח. חי עמך  ט. טוב  י. יובל  כ. כרם  ל. לתת לכם את ארץ כנען, להיות לכם לאלוקים  מ. מצבה, משכית  נ. נזיריה  ס. ספיחים  ע. עבודת עבד  פ. פרך  צ. צמיתות  ק. קרוב  ר. ראש השנה  ש. שופר  ת. תשע וארבעים

א     During the שמיטה year, one refrains from working the land and harvesting crops. According to most opinions, the mitzva of שמיטה today is a מצוה דרבנן.

שמיטה demonstrates faith in Hashem that all produce and crops in Eretz Yisrael are ultimately the result of Hashem's ברכות. Eretz Yisrael is the land that Benei Yisrael received as a ברכה from Hashem. If we do not keep the שמיטה, then we do not recognize where the source of our ברכות is from, and we are not worthy of living in Eretz Yisrael.

בחוקותי

א. אילני סרק ב. ברית ג. גשם ד. דבר ה. העשירי ו. והעמידו לפני הכהן והעריך אותו הכהן ז. זכר ח. חרבה ט. טוב ברע ורע בטוב י. ישן נושן כ. כופר בעיקר, כופר במצוות ל. לחם מ. מעשר שני נ. נדר ס. סילוק השכינה ע. עמלים בתורה פ. פרי בעתו צ. ציווי ק. קללות ר. רץ מפניהם ש. שלום ת. תוכחה

Eretz Yisrael will produce crops because there will be a lot of rain. Benei Yisrael will have a lot to eat and will dwell in Eretz Yisrael peacefully. Hashem will dwell among Benei Yisrael, and all of the nations will fear them.

במדבר

א. א' אייר ב. במדבר סיני באהל מועד ג. גלגולת ד. דגל ה. העדות ו. ולא יגעו אל הקודש ז. זכרים ח. חודש ט. טוב לצדיק טוב לשכנו י. יוצא צבא כ. כסוי עור ל. למשפחותם, לבית אבותם מ. מנורת המאור, מלקחיה, מחתותיה, מזבח הזהב נ. נשיאים ס. סביב למשכן ע. עשרים שנה פ. פקודים צ. צבא ק. קהת, קודש הקדשים ר. ראש לבית אבותם ש. שקל ת. תימנה

ל     Reuven, Shimon, Levi, Yehuda, Yissachar, Zevulun, Dan, Naftali, Gad, Asher, Yosef, Binyamin

מ   תכלת is a blue color. קריעת ים סוף, the splitting of the Red Sea, happened on the eighth day after Benei Yisrael came out of Mitzrayim; therefore, the eighth string on the tzitzit is blue to remind us of Kriyat Yam Suf. The Gemara says that when one sees the תכלת in the tzitzit he is reminded of the blue in the sea, which reminds us of the blue in the sky, which reminds us of the throne of Hashem in the שמים above. These reminders help a person adhere to the Torah.

**Parsha Puzzler**

Rashi explains that Hashem shows His love of Benei Yisrael by counting them, and this counting was right before the dedication of the Mishkan.

**Questions**

א. אלעזר ב. ברכת כהנים ג. גדל, גילה ד. דיבר, דיבורים ה. השקה ו. וישלחו אותם אל מחוץ למחנה ז. זג ח. חנוכת המזבח ט. טמא לנפש י. יין כ. כף אחת ל. לויים מ. מי המרים המאררים נ. נזיר, נדר ס. סל מצות ע. עגלה פ. פרע צ. צב ק. קרבן, קטורת ר. ראובן ש. שלשים ת. תער

ב   In preparation for the ברכת כהנים, the Kohen must remove his shoes and wash his hands. During ברכת כהנים, one should close his or her eyes and avoid looking directly at the Kohanim. Outside of Eretz Yisrael, ברכת כהנים is said only during תפילת מוסף on the festivals, unless the festival falls on Shabbat; but in Eretz Yisrael, ברכת כהנים is recited every day during שחרית, and during מוסף.

**Parsha Puzzler**

Rashi explains that יברכך means that one will be prosperous because his possessions will be blessed. וישמרך means that Hashem will protect his possessions from being stolen.

Questions

א. אל מול פני המנורה ב. ברית ה' ג. גר ד. דן ה. הראהו הקב"ה באצבע ו. ויהי בנסוע הארון ז. זכרנו את הדגה ח. חצוצרות ט. טל י. יורד כ. כסף ל. לקטו מ. מרים, מתלוננים נ. נבואה ס. סמיכה, סמיכה ע. ענו פ. פנים אל פנים צ. צפורה ק. קברות התאווה ר. רשעים ש. שליו ת. תקיעת החצוצרות

**ו** It is disrespectful to turn one's back to קדושה; therefore, upon leaving, he should not turn away from the ארון, but rather walk backward with his face toward the ארון.

**ט** Every morning in the מדבר, Benei Yisrael collected the מן that fell overnight. On Shabbat, Benei Yisrael were not allowed to collect the מן. Instead, they were told to collect two portions on Erev Shabbat. To remember the מן and the double portion Benei Yisrael had on Shabbat, we use לחם משנה, two loaves of bread or challa, for the Shabbat meal. Each loaf of the לחם משנה should be whole, and one holds the loaves together with both hands when making the ברכה of המוציא

**מ** הכרת הטוב means to appreciate good and to be grateful for the good that is done for you. Hashem created Chava for Adam because He did not want Adam to be lonely. This was a gift from Hashem to Adam. Yet after Adam ate from the tree of knowledge, and Hashem reproached him, he immediately blamed his sin on Chava. By doing so, Adam was ungrateful to Hashem.

Parsha Puzzler

The trumpets were used to gather Benei Yisrael, or to gather the leaders of Benei Yisrael, or as a sign for Benei Yisrael to pack up and get ready to travel to the next camp.

Questions

א. אנשים ב. באנו אל הארץ אשר שלחתנו ג. גוי גדול ד. דבת
הארץ ה. הפרשת חלה ו. ויהס ז. זבת חלב ודבש ח. חילול שבת
ט. טובה הארץ י. יהושע כ. כלב ל. לתור מ. מקושש, מחלל,
מות יומת נ. נתנה ראש ונשובה מצרימה ס. סלח נא לעון העם הזה,
סלחתי כדברך ע. ענקים פ. פתיל תכלת צ. ציצית ק. קרעו בגדיהם
ר. רגום ש. שוגג ת. תרי״ג

ד Eretz Yisrael is so small, yet it contains so much. The Golan can be cold and have fresh mountain air, while the Negev is hot and dry. Eretz Yisrael is the land of the שבעת המינים, the seven species that are products of the country.

ה Any dough made from grains requires הפרשת חלה, removal of a כזית measurement of dough. Prior to removing the measurement of dough, one should recite the ברכה: להפריש חלה. In the time of the Beit HaMikdash, the dough was given as a gift to a Kohen. Today, the dough is placed in the oven, burned, and then discarded.

ח There are thirty-nine מלאכות, or types of work, that were done in the Mishkan and are prohibited on Shabbat. מלאכות שבת are prohibited from the Torah. Examples of מלאכות are tearing, cooking, and planting.

פ, צ Any four-cornered garment requires tzitzit. The ברכה made on tzitzit is על מצות ציצית, and should be said prior to putting on the tzitzit. The mitzva of tzitzit applies only during the day. Boys should be taught to wear tzitzit even prior to their bar mitzva. Tzitzit can be made of cotton, but some opinions say they should be made of wool.

This question is discussed at length by many commentators. The Ramban explains that Moshe, just like any other general, wanted the מרגלים to simply find the best strategy of attack to conquer Eretz Yisrael. Moshe did not expect the מרגלים to give a negative report about Eretz Yisrael. The Ramban explains that Moshe expected the מרגלים to talk about how great Eretz Yisrael was, and, as leaders of Benei Yisrael, encourage them to conquer the land.

א. אבירם or און בן פלת ב. בני לוי ג. גורן ד. דתן ה. העדה ו. ויקח קרח ז. זר, זרע אהרן ח. חנטת הפרי ט. טלית שכולו תכלת י. יעקב כ. כל העדה כולם קדושים ל. לוי מ. מגיפה נ. נחלה ס. סורו ע. עדה פ. פצתה את פיה, פדיון הבן צ. ציץ ק. קהת ר. רב לכם בני לוי ש. שקלים ת. תרומה

> ט    A טלית גדול can be worn by anyone who is bar mitzva,
> thirteen years of age. However, today most people
> begin wearing one when they get married. The טלית
> גדול can be worn all day, but it is generally worn
> during שחרית. The ברכה on the טלית גדול is
> להתעטף בציצית. When one starts to wear a טלית גדול, he should
> not make a ברכה on the טלית קטן but rather have in
> mind during the ברכה on the טלית גדול to cover the
> ברכה on the טלית קטן as well.

> פ    The mitzva of פדיון הבן is required when a firstborn
> son is born to a Yisrael. The father must redeem the
> child by giving money to a Kohen as a gift. The פדיון
> הבן cannot be done until thirty days have passed
> since the son is born, and should be done right away
> on the thirty-first day.

A Yisrael must give a Kohen a portion of the fruit harvested every year. This portion is called תרומה גדולה. A Yisrael gives מעשר ראשון, one-tenth of all the new fruit, to the Levi, and the Levi then gives one-tenth of that fruit for תרומת מעשר, which goes to the Kohen.

Questions

א. אדומה ב. בשר, בגדים, במים ג. גבול ד. דרך המלך נלך ה. הר ההר ו. וירם משה את ידו ויך את הסלע במטהו פעמים ז. זאת חקת התורה ח. חרס ט. טיפות י. יאסף אהרן אל עמיו כי לא יבא אל הארץ כ. כל העדה ל. לא תעבור בי פן בחרב אצא לקראתך מ. מי מריבה נ. נחש, נחש נחושת ס. סיחון ע. ענני הכבוד פ. פרה אדומה צ. צין ק. קדש ר. רבים ש. שער שחור ת. תטמא עד הערב

Parsha Puzzler

This is one of the reasons why the Torah introduces the פרה אדומה as a חוק, a mitzva that we cannot completely understand. There are many concepts in the Torah one cannot understand; regardless, when he complies with them, he demonstrates dedication to Torah and mitzvot.

Questions

א. אולי אוכל נכה בו ב. בלעם ג. גרתיו ד. דוד ה. הן עם לבדד ישכן ו. ויחבש את אתנו ז. זקני מואב, זקני מדין ח. חמור ט. טלית י. יזל מים מדליו כ. כסף ל. לא תלך עמהם לא תאר את העם כי ברוך הוא מ. מה טובו אהליך יעקב נ. נסים ס. סביבותיהם ע. עם יצא ממצרים פ. פעור צ. ציפור ק. קסמים ר. רגל ש. שלש רגלים ת. תעשה, תדבר

>  מ    This פסוק describes the glory of the tents of Yaakov, which refers to the *batei kenesset* (synagogues) and *batei midrash*. Therefore, it is appropriate to recite this פסוק when one enters a *beit knesset* or *beit midrash* for the first time every day.

Parsha Puzzler

Benei Yisrael are members of a nation who remember their past in order to preserve their future. Rav Moshe Feinstein explains that Bilam understood this strength. Therefore, he described Benei Yisrael as coming out of Mitzrayim, because even though it had already happened, he knew that they would remind themselves of it every day. This is what provides Benei Yisrael with their special strength and resilience to continue.

א. אלעזר, אהרן ב. ברית שלום ג. גורל ד. דתן ואבירם ה. השבועות, הביכורים ו. ועניתם את נפשותיכם ז. זר ח. חג ט. טרחנין י. יהושע כ. כל מלאכת עבודה לא תעשו ל. למה יגרע שם אבינו מתוך משפחתו כי אין לו בן מ. מקושש עצים, מחלל שבת נ. נחלה ס. סמיכה ע. עצרת פ. פעור צ. צאן אשר אין להם רועה ק. קנא את קנאתי ר. ראש ש. שאו את ראש כל עדת בני ישראל ת. תרצה

> ו  Some of the things we must refrain from on Yom Kippur are eating and drinking, bathing, rubbing ourselves with oil, and wearing leather shoes. The main mitzva one performs on Yom Kippur is תשובה, repenting for all sins.

Rashi explains that the שבטים would criticize Pinchas for killing a נשיא and because his grandfather was married to Yitro's daughter, who had once worshiped עבודה זרה. Hashem wanted to ensure that Benei Yisrael would know that Pinchas was correct in what he did and was a great person. Therefore, the פסוק delineates his lineage, explaining that he comes directly from Aharon.

א. אלעזר ב. בגדים ג. גד ד. דיבון ה. הרגו בחרב ו. וימסרו ז. זכרים ח. חמש ט. טף י. יום שמעו כ. כלי זהב ל. לפני בני ישראל מ. מנשה נ. נדרים ס. סיחון ע. עוג פ. פנחס צ. צדיקים ק. קריתים ר. ראשי המטות ש. שבועה ת. תשובו

נ   If one makes a נדר, a vow, then he must fulfill it in order to avoid making a false oath. If it is impossible to fulfill the נדר, then he must do התרת נדרים, nullifying the נדר. It is customary to do התרת נדרים before Rosh HaShana in order to rid oneself of any oaths taken prior to the new year. התרת נדרים involves going in front of a בית דין, which can be made up of three men above the age of thirteen, and asking them to nullify the נדר with a special text found in the siddur. The congregation nullifies all נדרים they may have taken during the year, during the Kol Nidrei service.

 **Parsha Puzzler** Rashi explains that this teaches us that these five kings were all united and equally evil with regard to their attempt to destroy Benei Yisrael.

 **Questions**

א. אהרן, ארבעים שנה ב. בפתע, בלא איבה ג. גולה, גואל, גבול ד. דרום ה. הר ההר ו. והורשתם את הארץ וישבתם בה ז. זאת תהיה לכם הארץ לגבולותיה סביב ח. חסדיו ט. טרודים באבלם י. ירושה כ. כהן גדול ל. לויים מ. ממחרת הפסח נ. נחל מצרים ס. סין, סוכות ע. עיר מקלט פ. פי החירת צ. צו את בני ישראל ק. קברות התאווה ר. רוצח ש. שלש, שלש, שש ת. תחניפו, תטמא

ו   When one comes to live in Eretz Yisrael he is performing the mitzva of ישוב ארץ ישראל. Supporting Eretz Yisrael, working in the country, and settling the land are all part of the mitzva of dwelling in the Jewish homeland and reestablishing it as a ירושה, an inheritance.

Rashi explains that Hashem wanted to show His love for Benei Yisrael. Regardless of the fact that Benei Yisrael were punished and had to travel in the מדבר for many years, Hashem did not move them around from place to place too much and allowed them to rest for a long time at each stop. To demonstrate Hashem's kindness, the Torah mentions every place that Benei Yisrael traveled.

דברים

א. ואלה הדברים  ב. בעשתי עשר חדש באחד לחדש  ג. גבול  ד. דרך מדבר מואב  ה. הבו לכם אנשים חכמים  ו. ויפנו, ויעלו, ויבאו, וירגלו  ז. (די) זהב  ח. חזק  ט. טוב הדבר אשר דברת לעשות  י. ירושה  כ. כוכבי השמים  ל. לא אסור ימין ושמאל  מ. מלכי האמורי, מנחל ארנון עד נחל הר חרמן  נ. נהר פרת, נהר הגדול  ס. סיחן  ע. עוג,   עשתרת באדרעי פ. פליט – Palit comes from the word palat which means to escape. Og escaped from the war between Avraham Avinu and the five kings. צ. צדיקים  ק. קדש ברנע  ר. רפאים  ש. שלשים ושמונה שנה ת. תקרבון אלי ושמעתיו

דברים means words. Rashi explains that Moshe was about to reprimand Benei Yisrael for all of the mistakes they had made in the מדבר. In order to avoid embarrassing Benei Yisrael, the Torah uses the vague expression: "These are the *words* that Moshe spoke," without divulging what kind of words they are.

ואתחנן

א. אעברה נא ואראה  ב. בית המקדש  ג. גוי גדול  ד. דרך ארץ ה. הר הטוב  ו. וזאת התורה אשר שם משה  ז. זבת חלב ודבש  ח. חרמון ט. טוטפת  י. יד, ימין ושמאל  כ. כבד את אביך ואת אמך  ל. לפנים משורת הדין  מ. מזוזות  נ. נשל גוים רבים מפניך  ס. סמל  ע. עשרת הדברות  פ. פנים בפנים  צ. צפונה  ק. וקשרתם  ר. ראש הפסגה  ש. שמע אל החקים ואל המשפטים  ת. תוסיפו, תגרעו

ו  הגבהה means (to) lift. It is done every time the Torah is read from the scroll. The person performing it lifts the Torah up, revealing its print and the place where the reader of the Torah has read or will read from. Ashkenazim do הגבהה after reading from the Torah, and Sephardim do it prior to reading.

ט  Tefillin can be worn by anyone who is bar mitzva, thirteen years of age. The two parts of tefillin are the *shel yad*, worn on the forearm, and the *shel rosh*, worn on the front of the head. It is unclear whether these are considered two mitzvot or one. Because of this, there is a separate ברכה made on each, but one should refrain from talking until both ברכות are recited and both tefillin have been placed. The *shel yad* is placed first, and the ברכה one makes is להניח תפילין. Then the *shel rosh* is placed, and the ברכה recited is על מצות תפילין.

ל  When one buys an extra beautiful etrog or lulav for Sukkot that costs more money, it is הידור מצוה, beautifying the mitzva, and is לפנים משורת הדין.

מ  The mezuza is a parchment with the first chapter of קריאת שמע written on it. One places it on the right side of the doorpost as he or she enters a room. It is customary to kiss the mezuza as one passes through the doorway.

ת  Rashi explains that examples of transgressing בל תוסיף are if one took five species on Sukkot instead of four, or if one tied five strings for tzitzit together instead of four. If one took three species on Sukkot instead of four, one would transgress בל תגרע.

The word ואתחנן comes from the root word חנן, which means beseech. Moshe was referring to the time he asked Hashem to allow him to go into Eretz Yisrael after the war with Sichon and Og. Rashi explains that ואתחנן is a request made by someone when they do not feel they are worthy enough to make requests. Moshe did not feel worthy to ask Hashem for anything because of his modesty.

עקב

א. ארץ אשר לא במסכנות תאכל בה לחם, ארץ אשר אבניה ברזל ומהרריה תחצוב נחושת ב. ברוך ג. גר, גרים הייתם בארץ מצרים ד. דגנך ה. הכל בידי שמים חוץ מיראת שמים ו. ואכלת ושבעת וברכת ז. זכור לעבדיך לאברהם ליצחק וליעקב ח. חיל ט. טובה י. יורה כ. כחי ועצם ידי עשה לי את החיל הזה ל. לחם לא אכלתי ומים לא שתיתי מ. מצוה אתכם היום נ. נפש ס. סרו ע. עבודה שבלב פ. פסל לך צ. צרעה ק. קריאת שמע ר. רימון ש. שעורה ת. תלמוד תורה

---

ו    One says ברכת המזון only after he has eaten a כזית of bread. He should say the ברכה in the same room in which he made the ברכה of המוציא and ate his meal. He should not leave the table after eating until saying the ברכת המזון. As long as he is waiting at the table where he is eating, it is still permissible to say ברכת המזון, providing he does not allow seventy-two minutes to pass without eating or drinking anything.

---

ט    Eretz Yisrael is so small, yet it contains so much. The Golan can be cold and have fresh mountain air, while the Negev is hot and dry. Eretz Yisrael is the land of the שבעת המינים, the seven species that are products of the country.

---

ע    שחרית is the morning prayer which corresponds to the תמיד של שחר, morning sacrifice, offered in the Beit HaMikdash. One can pray שחרית (שמונה עשרה) from נץ החמה, the first ray of sunlight in the sky, which is a

שחרית special mitzva called *vatikin*. One should preferably finish praying שחרית by the end of four variable hours into the day. One must finish praying שחרית by חצות היום, midday. Once there is light in the sky, one should refrain from doing anything until praying שחרית. מנחה is the afternoon prayer. One can begin praying מנחה from half a variable hour after midday, and should complete מנחה by שקיעת החמה, or sunset. Once it is close to that time, one should avoid sitting down to have a meal with bread, lest he forget to pray. מעריב is the evening prayer. The ideal time for praying מעריב is after צאת הכוכבים, when it is dark outside. Although one can begin praying מעריב as early as one and one-quarter variable hours before sunset, if he does so, he must repeat the קריאת שמע after dark. מעריב begins with ברכו, and one should not talk from ברכו until after the שמונה עשרה is recited.

ק   One is obligated to recite קריאת שמע in the morning and at night. The first פסוק of קריאת שמע is "שמע ישראל, etc.," which is the way a person accepts Hashem and the responsibility of keeping the mitzvot. When one says קריאת שמע, he should concentrate on the fact that Hashem is the sole Creator of the universe. One should also be careful to say every single letter of קריאת שמע clearly, especially when the last letter of one word is the same as the first letter of the next word. For example, with the words בכל לבבך, one should be careful to pause in between the two words, so that the lameds do not cause the two words to sound like one.

ר, ש   The שבעת המינים are wheat, barley, grapes (wine), figs, pomegranates, olives, and dates. The ברכה אחרונה on products made of wheat or barley such as bread, is ברכת המזון. On cake or crackers made from wheat or barley the ברכה אחרונה is על המחיה, or מעין

שלש. The ברכה אחרונה on wine is על הגפן, or מעין שלש, and on the rest of the fruits it is על העץ, or מעין שלש. If one were going to eat from all of the שבעת המינים, he or she would first say the ברכה of בורא מיני מזונות on the wheat (which would also cover the barley), then the ברכה of בורא פרי הגפן on the wine, and finally, the ברכה of בורא פרי העץ on the olives (having in mind the rest of the fruit; this ברכה would cover the rest of the fruit). If there were grapes instead of wine, then one would make the ברכה of בורא פרי העץ on the olives and have in mind the rest of the fruit.

**Parsha Puzzler**

The Gemara asks this question and explains that by learning Torah and supporting Torah study one fulfills this mitzva of clinging to Hashem.

ראה

**Questions**

א. אבד תאבדון ב. ברכה ג. גרויים ד. דם ה. השמר לך פן תעלה עולותיך בכל מקום אשר תראה ו. ועברתם את הירדן, וישבתם בארץ אשר ה׳ אלקיכם מנחיל אתכם, והניח לכם מכל אויביכם מסביב, וישבתם בטח, ובו תדבקון ז. זכר ח. חולם החולם ט. טמא, טהור י. ירושלים כ. כופר בכל התורה כולה ל. לא תבשל גדי בחלב אמו מ. מפרסת פרסה, שוסעת שסע נ. נביא שקר ס. סנפיר, קשקשת ע. עיבל פ. פתוח תפתח את ידך צ. צדקה ק. קדוש, קדש את עצמך במה שמותר לך ר. רגלים, ריקם ש. שילה ת. תתגדדו, תשימו קרחה בין עיניכם למת

ל  In a kosher home, to separate between meat and milk we have separate sets of dishes, separate countertops, and many people have separate cupboards and sinks. There are different customs regarding waiting between meat and milk. Some people wait one hour, some wait three hours, and some wait into the sixth hour. The most popular and most accepted custom is to wait six hours. If one eats milk products and wants to eat meat, he must first wipe and rinse out his mouth. This process is called קינוח and הדחה. Brushing teeth is an acceptable way to fulfill this requirement.

פ, צ The most popular way to give צדקה is by giving poor people money, but there are many other ways to fulfill this mitzva. One can provide poor people with clothing, food, or services. The best form of צדקה is providing someone with a job. It is also preferable to give צדקה anonymously, and to avoid revealing where the צדקה came from. This way the poor person does not get embarrassed that he is receiving help from others.

The Ibn Ezra explains that a prophet may claim to have had a vision while he was awake. The word dreamer refers to someone who claims to have had a vision in his sleep. Either a prophet or a dreamer can be false, and if they are, then they are חייב מיתה, liable to be punished by the death penalty.

שופטים

א. אשרה  ב. בין דם לדם, בין דין לדין, ובין נגע לנגע, דברי ריבות בשעריך; בנה בית חדש  ג. גג  ד. דגן  ה. השגת גבול  ו. והוצאת את האיש ההוא או את האשה ההיא אשר עשו את הדבר הרע הזה אל שעריך את האיש או את האשה וסקלתם באבנים ומתו  ז. זהב, זומם  ח. חמס  ט. טף  י. ימין שמאל ושמאל ימין  כ. כי האדם עץ השדה  ל. לא עץ למאכל הוא  מ. מצבה  נ. נטע כרם  ס. סוסים  ע. עדים זוממים  פ. פן ידרוף גואל הדם  צ. צדק צדק תרדף  ק. קוסם  ר. רוצח  ש. שופטים ושוטרים  ת. תמים תהיה עם ה' אלקיך

By making a statement like this one, the Sifri is emphasizing the importance of listening to the חכמים. There are sure to be times when one thinks that he knows better than the חכמים, but if people decide to make their own decisions it destroys the authority of Chazal and, ultimately, the foundation of the Torah.

א. אשת יפת תואר ב. בן סורר ומורה ג. גבר ד. דומה ה. השמר בנגע הצרעת לשמר מאד ו. ולעשות ככל אשר יורו אתכם הכהנים ז. זכור זכירת עמלק, זכירת מעשה מרים ח. חמור, חרישה ט. טבתם י. יבום כ. כלאים ל. לא תטה משפט מ. מעקה נ. נשך ס. סורר ומורה, סר מן הדרך ע. עמון ומואב פ. פשתן צ. צמר ק. קבור תקברנו ביום ההוא ר. ראשית אנו ש. שלוח הקן ת. תמחה את זכר עמלק

ק כבוד המת, showing respect to the dead, is extremely important. Some of the ways one fulfills this mitzva is by conducting a טהרה, purifying and cleaning the body before burial, wrapping the person who died with the טלית he used when he was alive, ensuring that the burial is done as quickly as possible, and escorting the person to be buried. The Mishna in Tractate Pe'ah says that escorting someone to burial is a mitzva that knows no bounds. The חברה קדישא is a group of people in every Jewish community who prepare a person for burial and conduct the טהרה.

There are four types of כלאים mentioned in the parsha. כלאי כרם and כלאי שדה are mix-breed fruits from the fields. One cannot mix two different species of animals to work together under one yoke. One cannot wear wool and flax together as a garment.

א. ארמי אובד אבי ב. בוכות ג. גרזיזם ד. דלקת ה. הרי זו ביכורים ו. ונצעק אל ה׳ אלקי אבתינו ז. זנב ח. חטא ט. טנא י. יקימך ה׳ לו לעם קדוש כ. כיבוש הארץ ל. לבן, לעקור מ. מקלה, מזלול נ. נגפים ס. סיחון ע. עיבל פ. פחד צ. צאן ק. קדחת ר. ראשית ש. שבעת המינים ת. תרומה

ברוך אתה בבואך, etc. Rashi explains that this means one should leave this world without sin just like he entered this world. Hashem promises to give over the enemies to Benei

Yisrael. The Torah says that Hashem will open His treasure house for Benei Yisrael, which refers to the rain that Hashem will provide in Eretz Yisrael.

א. אהבת ה' ב. ביום מותו, ברית ג. גוים, גילולים ד. דורות העתידים ה. הביאך ו. וירשתה והיטבך והרבך מאבתיך ז. זקנים ח. חטב עציך ט. טף י. יורש כ. כי קרוב אליך הדבר מאד ל. לא בשמים היא מ. משה נ. נשים ס. סדום ע. עמורה פ. פן יש בכם...שרש פרה ראש ולענה צ. צרת גלותם ק. קיבצך ר. ראשי ש. שבטיכם ת. תשובה

According to the Gemara and Rashi, the commandment refers to the mitzva of תלמוד תורה. According to the Ramban, the commandment refers to the mitzva of תשובה. Some commentators explain that both these opinions are one and the same and that the main way to do תשובה is by learning Torah. Both of these concepts go hand in hand, and one needs to incorporate them into his life regularly.

א. אהל מועד ב. באזני כל קהל ישראל ג. גר ד. דברים ה. הקהל ו. וילך משה ז. זרעם ח. חזק ואמץ ט. טף י. יהושע, ירדן כ. כי אביאנו אל האדמה אשר נשבעתי לאבתיו ל. למען ישמעו ולמען ילמדו ויראו את ה' מ. מאה ועשרים שנה נ. נשים ס. סוכות ע. ענן פ. (על) פתח האהל צ. צרות ק. קרא אל יהושע ר. רע בעיני ה' ש. שמיטה ת. תקרא את התורה הזאת

Rav Yonasan Eyebeshitz explains that the reason for the שמיטה year was in order for people to stop working their fields so that they could learn Torah. הקהל, reading the Torah in front of Benei Yisrael, reminded the people of their obligation to continue learning Torah regularly, even though the שמיטה year was over and they were now returning to work their fields.

**Questions**

א. אבות ב. בקר ג. גוים ד. דבש ה. ה לה׳ תגמלו זאת ו. וינאץ
מכעס בניו ובנתיו ז. זקניך ח. חכמים ט. חכמים י. ימצאהו בארץ מדבר
כ. כנשר ל. לא דבר ריק הוא מכם מ. מים (מטר) נ. נבו ס. סלע
ע. עלי דשא, עלי עשב פ. פעלו צ. צור ק. קיימים לעולם ר. רביבים
ש. שדי ת. תנובות

**Parsha Puzzler**

Rashi explains that Moshe was making a covenant between Benei Yisrael and Hashem. Moshe wanted a covenant that would last forever, so he chose witnesses like the שמים and ארץ that would always be present to confirm the covenant that was made.

**Questions**

א. איש האלקים ב. ברכה, בני ישראל ג. גרש ירחים ד. דבאך ה. הים
האחרון ו. ולא קם נביא עוד בישראל כמשה ז. זבולן ח. חפף עליו כל
היום ט. טבל בשמן רגלו י. יהושע כ. כנרת ל. לא ידע איש את קברתו
עד היום הזה מ. מואב, מול בית פעור נ. נשיקה ס. סמיכה ע. עבד ה׳
פ. פנים אל פנים צ. צדק ק. קבר ר. רוח חכמה ש. שלשים ת. תמרים

**Parsha Puzzler**

There are a number of answers given to this question. The Gemara says that Yehoshua wrote the last few פסוקים. A different opinion in the Gemara says that Moshe shed tears before he died, and the tears formed the words of the last few פסוקים in the Torah.

# *Glossary* מונחון

| | |
|---|---|
| *shoham* stones (onyx) | אבני שוהם |
| bundle of hyssop | אגודת אזוב |
| Tent of Meeting | אהל מועד |
| *Urim* and *Tumim* | אורים ותומים |
| unity | אחדות |
| ram | איל |
| prohibition | איסור |
| Egyptian man | איש מצרי |
| faith in Hashem | אמונה בה' |
| prohibited | אסור |
| apron-like garment | אפוד |
| locusts | ארבה |
| the four species | ארבעת המינים |
| Ark | ארון |
| earth | ארץ |
| garment | בגד |

| | |
|---:|---:|
| gold garments | בגדי זהב |
| garments worn by the Kohen | בגדי כהונה |
| clothes | בגדים |
| the search for leavened food before Pesach | בדיקת חמץ |
| pit | בור |
| faith | בטחון |
| belief | בטחון |
| *Bikurim,* first fruits | ביכורים |
| between man and his fellow | בין אדם לחברו |
| between man and God | בין אדם למקום |
| burning the leavened food before Pesach | ביעור חמץ |
| Jewish court | בית דין |
| birthright | בכורה |
| children of the Tribe of Gad | בני גד |
| children of the Tribe of Reuven | בני ראובן |
| hail | ברד |
| covenant | ברית |
| Covenant Between the Parts | ברית בין הבתרים |
| circumcision | ברית מילה |
| blessing | ברכה |
| blessing after eating | ברכה אחרונה |
| blessing before eating | ברכה ראשונה |
| blessings | ברכות |
| Grace After Meals | ברכת המזון |
| priestly blessings | ברכת כהנים |
| redemption | גאולה |
| redeeming a field | גאולת השדה |
| a holy nation | גוי קדוש |

| | |
|---|---|
| foreign nations | גוים |
| exile | גלות |
| convert | גר |
| stranger | גר |
| divorcee | גרושה |
| materialism | גשמיות |
| words | דברים |
| Generation of the Flood | דור המבול |
| speech | דיבור |
| blood | דם |
| knowledge | דעת |
| *derech eretz*, proper behavior | דרך ארץ |
| the way of Hashem | דרך ה׳ |
| lifting the Torah | הגבהה |
| showing appreciation | הכרת הטוב |
| blessing recited before eating bread | המוציא |
| separating challa from the dough | הפרשת חלה |
| that which is designated for a holy purpose | הקדש |
| gathering the people | הקהל |
| returning lost items | השבת אבידה |
| absolving vows | התרת נדרים |
| love your peer as you would yourself | ואהבת לרעך כמוך |
| merits | זכויות |
| elders | זקנים |
| elders of Moav | זקני מואב |
| performing mitzvot with alacrity | זריזין מקדימין למצוות |
| sprinkling of the blood | זריקת הדם |
| Jewish burial society | חברה קדישא |

| | |
|---|---|
| Destruction of the Temple | חורבן הבית |
| breastplate | חושן |
| breastplate of judgment | חושן משפט |
| the sin of the Golden Calf | חטא העגל |
| desecration of the Shabbat | חילול שבת |
| wise men | חכמים |
| leavened food | חמץ |
| kindness | חסד |
| trumpets | חצוצרות |
| decrees | חוקים |
| impure | טמא |
| impure as a result of contact with the dead | טמא מת |
| Jubilee | יובל |
| the sixth day | יום הששי |
| wine | יין |
| the Red (Reed) Sea | ים סוף |
| the Exodus from Egypt | יציאת מצרים |
| fear of Heaven (Hashem) | יראת שמים |
| inheritance | ירושה |
| settling in the Land of Israel | ישוב ארץ ישראל |
| respect | כבוד |
| respect for the deceased | כבוד המת |
| intent | כוונה |
| it was good | כי טוב |
| respecting one's parents | כיבוד אב ואם |
| washing basin | כיור |
| mixed breeding | כלאים |
| utensils used in the Tabernacle | כלי המשכן |

| | |
|---:|---:|
| utensils | כלים |
| covering the blood | כסוי הדם |
| cover | כפורת |
| Cherubs | כרובים |
| multicolored cloak | כתנת פסים |
| Tablets of the Covenant | לוחות הברית |
| two loaves of bread | לחם משנה |
| studying Torah | לימוד תורה |
| out of respect for Shabbat | לכבוד שבת |
| beyond the letter of the law | לפנים משורת הדין |
| slander | לשון הרע |
| the Flood | מבול |
| desert | מדבר |
| positive attributes | מדות טובות |
| sacrifices his/her life | מוסר נפש |
| He who drops the dew | מוריד הטל |
| Altar | מזבח |
| Gold Altar | מזבח הזהב |
| Outer Altar | מזבח החיצון |
| Altar for the Olah Sacrifice | מזבח העולה |
| one who desecrates the Shabbat | מחלל שבת |
| half-shekel | מחצית השקל |
| staff | מטה |
| attribute | מידה |
| plagues | מכות |
| selling leavened food before Pesach | מכירת חמץ |
| the plague of the firstborn | מכת בכורות |
| plague of lice | מכת כינים |

| | |
|---|---|
| angel | מלאך |
| an angel of Hashem | מלאך ה׳ |
| Angel of Death | מלאך המוות |
| work | מלאכה |
| angels | מלאכים |
| the War with Amalek | מלחמת עמלק |
| King of Israel | מלך ישראל |
| kingdom | מלכות |
| kingdom of the House of David | מלכות בית דוד |
| manna | מן |
| Menora | מנורה |
| sacrificing of one's life | מסירת נפש |
| eastern side of the Jordan River | מעבר לירדן |
| Evening Prayer | מעריב |
| tenth | מעשר |
| split hooves | מפריס פרסה |
| matza | מצה |
| commandments from the Torah | מצוות דאורייתא |
| rabbinic commandments | מצוות דרבנן |
| skin disease | מצורע |
| ritual bath | מקוה |
| one who gathers wood | מקושש עצים |
| spies | מרגלים |
| laws | משפטים |
| receiving the Torah | מתן תורה |
| gift | מתנה |
| prophets of Hashem | נביאי ה׳ |
| false prophets | נביאי הבעל |

| | |
|---|---|
| vows | נדרים |
| Jewish celibate / nazarite | נזיר |
| damages | נזק |
| portion | נחלה |
| washing the hands | נטילת ידיים |
| giants | נפילים |
| Leader / prince | נשיא |
| leaders / princes | נשיאים |
| interest | נשך |
| a woman suspected of adultery | סוטה |
| counting the *Omer* | ספירת העומר |
| the tradition of *teruma* | סרך תרומה |
| a servant of Hashem | עבד ה' |
| a Jewish servant | עבד עברי |
| service | עבודה |
| idolatry | עבודה זרה |
| serving Hashem | עבודת ה' |
| Golden Calf | עגל הזהב |
| Korach's group | עדת קרח |
| skins | עורות |
| evil eye | עין הרע |
| afflictions | עינוים |
| people of the land | עם הארץ |
| clouds of glory | ענני הכבוד |
| Tree of Knowledge | עץ הדעת |
| tree of the field | עץ השדה |
| Binding of Yitzchak | עקידת יצחק |
| cities of refuge | ערי מקלט |

| | |
|---:|---:|
| herbage | עשב |
| the Ten Commandments | עשרת הדברות |
| the ten days of penitence | עשרת ימי תשובה |
| redemption of the firstborn son | פדיון הבן |
| exempt | פטור |
| not valid | פסול |
| verse | פסוק |
| beginning section of the morning prayer service | פסוקי דזמרא |
| idol | פסל |
| red heifer | פרה אדומה |
| partition | פרוכת |
| Torah portion of Vaera | פרשת וארא |
| righteous person | צדיק |
| charity | צדקה |
| righteous woman | צדקת |
| modesty | צניעות |
| frogs | צפרדע |
| leprosy | צרעת |
| holiness | קדושה |
| be holy | קדושים |
| incense | קטורת |
| sanctifying the new month | קידוש החודש |
| prayer recited over the new moon | קידוש לבנה |
| curses | קללות |
| sacrifice | קרבן |
| *Asham* Sacrifice | קרבן אשם |
| *Chatat* Sacrifice (offered after someone sins) | קרבן חטאת |

| | |
|---|---|
| Musaf Sacrifice | קרבן מוסף |
| Mincha Sacrifice | קרבן מנחה |
| Olah Sacrifice | קרבן עולה |
| Omer Sacrifice | קרבן עומר |
| Pesach Sacrifice | קרבן פסח |
| Shlamim Sacrifice | קרבן שלמים |
| Todah Sacrifice | קרבן תודה |
| Tamid Sacrifice | קרבן תמיד |
| sacrifices | קרבנות |
| recital of the Shema prayer | קריאת שמע |
| Shema prayer recited before going to sleep | קריאת שמע על המיטה |
| the parting of the Reed Sea | קריעת ים סוף |
| rainbow | קשת |
| increase (interest) | רבית |
| the spirit of Shabbat | רוח שבת |
| spirituality | רוחניות |
| mercy | רחמנות |
| gossip | רכילות |
| wicked person | רשע |
| wicked people | רשעים |
| leaven | שאור |
| the Tribe of Efraim | שבט אפרים |
| the Tribe of Binyamin | שבט בנימין |
| the Tribe of Dan | שבט דן |
| the Tribe of Yehuda | שבט יהודה |
| the Tribe of Levi | שבט לוי |
| the Tribe of Menashe | שבט מנשה |
| the Tribe of Shimon | שבט שמעון |

| | |
|---:|---:|
| tribes | שבטים |
| the Seven Species (of Israel) | שבעת המינים |
| policemen | שוטרים |
| chew cud | שוסעת שסע |
| judges | שופטים |
| shofar | שופר |
| Satan | שטן |
| old age | שיבה |
| the song recited after the parting of the Reed Sea | שירת הים |
| beer | שכר |
| peace in the home | שלום בית |
| table | שלחן |
| *Amida* prayer of eighteen blessings | שמונה עשרה |
| *Shmita* | שמיטה |
| heaven | שמים |
| observing the mitzvot | שמירת המצוות |
| anointing oil | שמן המשחה |
| *shatnez* | שעטנז |
| flying, teeming creature | שרץ עוף |
| the two breads | שתי הלחם |
| Torah of Israel | תורת ישראל |
| settler | תושב |
| ark | תיבה |
| Moshe's ark | תיבת משה |
| blue dye | תכלת |
| studying Torah | תלמוד תורה |
| scholar | תלמיד חכם |

| | |
|---|---|
| prayer | תפילה |
| Prayer for Dew | תפילת טל |
| Afternoon Prayer | תפילת מנחה |
| Evening Prayer | תפילת ערבית |
| Morning Prayer | תפילת שחרית |
| portion | תרומה |
| donations | תרומות |
| penitence | תשובה |
| fill in | תשלומין |

# About the Author

**R**abbi Shalom Hammer has lived in Israel for twenty-five years. He served in the Rabbinate Division of the Israeli Defense Forces, helped establish and taught in Yeshivat Hesder Kiryat Gat, and currently serves as a lecturer for the IDF and Machane Meshutaf to help motivate troops in all divisions and infuse the Israeli army with Jewish identity and ideology. In addition, he founded Makom Meshutaf, an organization which advocates tolerance and unity between religious and secular Jews in Israel, promoting Jewish values and traditions in an open and comfortable environment. www.makommeshutaf.com

Rabbi Hammer has authored four books. His most recent book, *Derash Yehonatan*, is available from Maggid Books.

Rabbi Hammer is a contributing writer for *The Jerusalem Post* and is a renowned guest lecturer for communities throughout the Diaspora, including the United States, the United Kingdom, South Africa, and Australia. www.rabbihammer.com

*Maggid Books*
*The best of contemporary Jewish thought from*
*Koren Publishers Jerusalem Ltd.*